HOW TO REDESIGN YOUR YARD AND GARDEN

(previously published as MAKE YOUR GARDEN NEW AGAIN)

Stanley Schuler

*How to Redesign
Your Yard
and Garden*

How to Redesign Your Yard and Garden

(previously published as
MAKE YOUR GARDEN NEW AGAIN)

STANLEY SCHULER

HAWTHORN BOOKS, INC.
Publishers/NEW YORK

All photographs are by the author unless noted otherwise. Some were taken for an earlier book, *America's Great Private Gardens.*

Library of Congress Catalog Card Number: 76–20851

ISBN: 0–8015–3746–0

Published by arrangement with Simon and Schuster.

Contents

Sizing Up
1 What Needs to Be Done and How to Do It

It's an odd fact: there is more remodeling of gardens than building of new ones, and the processes are quite different. Yet when you look for information on how to relandscape and replant a garden in order to make it more attractive and functional or in order to add a new feature, it's hard to find.

Here comes help at last.

My No. 3 daughter and her husband were the first to make me understand that it was needed. They had just bought a thirty-year-old house surrounded by a scant acre of grass, good-sized trees and a hideous above-ground swimming pool, and we were discussing what should be done to the property.

"What we want to know is where to begin," Cary said.

"First thing I'm going to do is cut down those big hemlocks that make the study wing so dark," Charlie said.

"Agreed," Cary said. "But after that—you want a vegetable garden. And I want flowers. The foundation planting is a mess. And we're going to have to find a space to put a trolley for Jason. And that pool has to go—or else we should find a place where we can hide it and use it." She turned to me again. "But where do we start? This isn't like making a brand-new garden on a lot that doesn't have trees; that has only those few scrawny shrubs that builders always put in. With a new place you're starting from scratch and can do just about as you want. But here we're sort of locked in by what's already been done. There are a lot of plants that are too good to throw out but that are in the wrong places. And there are a lot of poor plants that are so big you can't afford to get rid of them either. So what do we do? Where, I want to know, do we start?"

I was about to answer, "Well, I've given you every book I ever wrote, and you'll find the answers there." And then I realized that that wasn't exactly true. I don't know of any garden books—mine included—that spell out how you go about doing over a garden; and I have no explanation for the lack. But what I do know is that garden remodeling is as common as house remodeling (about which many books have been written) and probably even more common. Why? Because there are more reasons for undertaking it.

For example, ever since my wife and I bought our home five years ago we've been doing over the garden; and we'll undoubtedly continue for some years to come. It was a beautiful garden when we took possession, but it wasn't quite everything we wanted. The previous owner had a large parking area that we didn't need, so we tore it out and put in a vegetable garden. We are continually replacing plants with species we like better. We're contemplating the unhappy necessity of cutting down a towering sycamore that is causing foundation leaks and ruining the paint at one end of the house. And sooner or later we know we're going to have to take steps to reduce our many lawn areas in order to make mowing and leaf-raking less onerous.

Our No. 1 daughter and her husband remodeled their first garden extensively because, although it was ten years old, the planting was sparse and ugly. They wanted something more attractive and they also desperately needed shade. Now, having recently moved to a much older home, they are remodeling their garden to save innumerable fine plants that are in danger of being crowded out. In addition, they should redesign and rebuild the terrace, which is an abomination. And they must figure out a way to cope with the water that floods the big, sunny, low spot where their children like to play.

No. 2 daughter and her husband also have had two homes, both with gardens that required remodeling. The first had too many flower beds and not enough lawn area. The second has too much of everything except beauty.

And then there are our friends John and Happy White. In thirty-five years they have owned three homes, and in every case they have completely torn apart and rebuilt both house and garden. Ask them why, and they'll give you a long list of practical and esthetic reasons. But one of the main reasons, I'm sure, is that they simply enjoy the challenge. They are the last people I can think of who will need this book.

But for Cary and Charlie, Ashley and Tom, Randy and Bill, and the thousands upon thousands of other families who buy or own old properties, garden remodeling is usually a bit frightening and puzzling. Hopefully, it won't be that way any longer.

There are two types of garden remodeling. They are the same as the two types of house remodeling. One is called "making alterations," the other "making additions." As a rule, making alterations involves making some additions: and making additions involves some alterations. Nevertheless the majority of remodeling projects have a distinct leaning one way or the other.

Making alterations in a garden is essentially a changing-around process. The job may be done just once—usually fairly soon after a family buys an "old" house. (I put "old" in quotation marks because any house that has been occupied—even for only a year—is an old house.) Or it may be stretched out over a long period of time.

On the other hand, making an addition to a garden is almost always a one-shot undertaking of considerable magnitude which may be followed in subsequent years by other one-shot undertakings also of considerable magnitude.

Since the gardening industry, unlike the building industry, makes no attempt to find out what is happening to residential properties in the United States, I have no way of knowing whether more gardens are altered or added to in any given year. Before World War II, alterations predominated. But since then the American attitude toward the garden has changed. It is no longer just a pretty thing to be looked at. Now it is mainly a thing to be lived in and used. Consequently more and more homeowners are adding terraces, swimming pools, play areas, parking areas, and other such utilitarian spaces. And because of this strong trend, it is altogether possible that additions today outnumber alterations.

Be that as it may, the first part of this book deals mainly with making alterations in a garden, because this is usually the first kind of remodeling that homeowners undertake.

The plain fact of the matter is that most established gardens need considerable remodeling. This is especially true of those more than about eight years old, because it takes that length of time for the little shrubs and trees put in by developers to grow large enough to start to darken windows and crowd front walks. In other words, overgrown plants—a product of age—are the primary reason that gardens need face-lifting. But they are only one reason. I can point out many hundred- and two-hundred-year-old gardens that are not overgrown in the least but that need remodeling because they require too much maintenance or are not arranged to suit the needs and living habits of the modern family. And there are also many two- and three-year-old gardens that need remodeling simply because they are badly laid out.

Whatever your garden's deficiencies may be, you shouldn't undertake its remodeling without having observed the following precautions.

Give it time to reveal itself. This doesn't mean that, if it has obvious serious faults, you should delay making changes in it. Much to the horror of the people from whom they had bought the place, Cary and Charlie cut down the hemlocks that darkened their house less than a week after they moved in; and they were absolutely right in doing so. But in most situations it's advisable to wait for spring and summer to roll around to show you the bulbs, perennials and ferns that the garden contains. True, those that appear may not be worth saving. But if they are worth saving, your delay in tearing into the garden may have saved them from destruction. And it may also have kept you from spending money on new plants you don't need.

Another reason for delaying the start of remodeling until warm weather arrives is to give you a chance to make positive identification of the deciduous trees, shrubs and vines in the garden. Many of these are difficult to pinpoint when they are bare. Yet it sometimes happens that sad-looking winter specimens that you might be tempted to tear out turn into lovely summer specimens, while good winter specimens turn out to be full of problems in summer.

Make sure your picture of your garden is clear. It's amazing how many homeowners have only half-accurate mental images of their properties. For instance, an owner may not know the precise location of his lot lines. Or he may not know where his septic tank and disposal field are. Or he may not know whether a given area is in shade three, six or nine hours a day. Or he may not even know whether his house faces south or west.

Ignorance and mistaken ideas are not conducive to successful garden remodeling. A friend of mine is a case in point. For some reason he was unaware that the local water company had a right-of-way running through his lot and that it had installed in this a pipeline carrying water to an adjoining lot. So when he was changing some planting, he moved several trees into the right-of-way. As luck would have it, they flourished. And then one day a representative of the water company appeared at the door. "Mr. Marshfield," he announced, "we're going to have to put in a new main to the Mulligans—the old one is clogged. We'll do what we can to save those trees of yours, of course, but if we can't—well, we're sorry."

Only one of the trees survived.

The moral is obvious. Before you begin to remodel your garden, study it at length—on the ground and in the legal descriptions—to make sure you can do what you want to do and without later repercussions.

Determine in which climate zone you live. This is easy to do and very important. Just turn to the Plant Hardiness Zone Map on page 20, establish the location of your town, and note which climate zone it is in. (If it's on a borderline between zones, you should figure that you live in the zone with the lower number.) From then on, whenever you buy, beg or propagate new plants, you should make certain that they will survive and grow in your zone.

Most current garden books and some plant catalogs indicate the climate zones for every plant described. This information is given in various ways. For example:

Scotch pine—Zone 2 southward
Scotch pine—Hardy to Zone 2
Scotch pine—Zone 2

But unfortunately none of these descriptions indicates how far south Scotch pine (or any other plant) will grow. That is why in this book I give both the northern and southern limits for each plant. For example:

Scotch pine—Zones 2–8

White oak—Zones 5–10

Mountain andromeda—Zones 5–9

Common lilac—Zones 3b–8

Mugo pine—Zones 2–8a

In other words, if you live in Zones 2, 3, 4, 5, 6, 7 or 8, you should be able to grow Scotch pine. But if you live in Zones 1, 9 or 10, you cannot. (Note that if the letter "a" or "b" is added to a zone number, it indicates that the plant in question will grow in only part of the zone. The letter "a" stands for the northern half of the zone, "b" for the southern. The common lilac, for instance, will grow in only the southern, warmer half of Zone 3. Mugo pine, on the other hand, will grow only in the northern, colder half of Zone 8.)

Be sure you know what you're trying to do and that what you do will contribute to the beauty of the garden. Making changes in a garden involves work and money, so it's a foolish waste to do anything that doesn't fulfill a purpose. This is obvious—although the obvious is often ignored.

Handsome shrub and tree planting is projected from the corner of the house to block the view from the street of the living room and inner part of the raised terrace. The planting includes a pair of arborvitaes, rhododendrons and a flowering dogwood.

OPPOSITE

The property shown in this picture and the following four pictures has been undergoing remodeling ever since it was purchased about ten years ago. Situated on a busy street corner, it is owned by a woman who loves gardening and wants to share her work with passersby but who still wishes to retain her privacy. The fence surrounding the garden keeps people out; the seemingly casual planting of trees and shrubs keeps them from peering into the windows.

One of the flower borders—planted mostly to perennials—is just inside the fence. Roses grow under the pergola, which was designed purely for ornament. Large evergreens once stood where the perennial border bulges out into the lawn. Their place has been taken by the old apple tree referred to in Chapter 5.

But just having a purpose is not enough. The end result must be an asset, not a liability, to the garden. This is where garden-remodeling projects often go astray.

One of my friends in California went to great lengths some years ago to improve the landscaping in front of her newly purchased home in the Los Angeles area. One of her primary aims was to screen the house from the nearby street. This is a laudable idea, but she chose to accomplish it in a strange way—by planting two redwoods on either side of the doorway and within 20 feet of the house wall.

"Why redwoods?" I asked.

"I love 'em," she answered. "I grew up with them in northern California and I want to make them grow down here too."

"But don't you think they'll be a little big?"

"Oh, I'm not worried about that," she said airily. And I dropped the subject.

Today the house is hidden. The front rooms are dark. The yard resembles a jungle even though it has only two trees.

Don't go too far too fast. Admittedly, this is not always possible. When you move into a house that is so surrounded with shrubs and trees that the paint is peeling, the roof is covered with moss and the interior feels and even smells like a dank dungeon, drastic action must be taken at once. But when more modest alterations seem called for, take your time, feel your way. You may find that fewer and smaller changes are all you need.

This was brought home to me more forcefully when we started work on our present garden. Our principal flower beds were (and are) two long, narrow rectangles separated by a walk. At the end was a paved circle with a semicircular fence screening the entire area from the road. The fence was an eyesore. A stockade type made of small half-rounds with pointed tops, it was unpainted, very tired-looking, and with no planting in front to relieve it. My wife and I vowed it had to come down. But before going to work on it we had to decide what to put in its place. There were several possibilities, but none overwhelmed us. Meanwhile there were other more urgent things to be done. So we let the matter slide.

Then one day Elizabeth had an idea: "If we can't settle on what to do, why don't we just paint the old fence white? Maybe that will at least take the curse off it till we get a better idea."

She was wrong. The transformation was positively amazing. We liked the fence so well that we planted a pair of Hicks yews in front of it; and I doubt now that we'll ever bother to replace it. Not that it's perfect, but it's better than good enough.

The experience of a neighboring family turned out less happily, but it also proves the wisdom of not rushing into garden remodeling. These neighbors are a youngish couple and know little about gardening. But when they moved into their new old home, they were full of enthusiasm and almost immediately undertook to turn a high, steep bank facing the kitchen and dining room into a rock garden.

Unfortunately there are few projects for which novice gardeners are less qualified, and this one turned out predictably. The rock garden was dreadful, and I am certain the couple knew it, because they haven't gone near it since. So what was meant to be the prime feature of the property is now its greatest defect—all because the owners tried to go too far too fast.

A *"before and after" example of a very recent change. Because of an overhanging swamp maple, the corner to the left of the driveway entrance used to be so dark that even hostas struggled to survive. So the tree was cut down and replaced by a flowering dogwood. This not only opened up the area and permitted a better view of the house but also replaced an inferior, "dirty" tree with one of our very best species.*

If you need professional help, get the right kind. This will depend on whether your project is limited to the selection and planting of plants or whether it involves the rearrangement, redesign and redevelopment of the entire garden or a rather sizable part of it.

If you're simply concerned with plants, a Gardener with a capital G or a nurseryman should be able to give you adequate help. But unfortunately Gardeners—usually men who came to this country from England, Italy or Japan—have just about disappeared from the scene. So that leaves you with the nurserymen.

A nurseryman is a person who owns a nursery in which he raises trees, shrubs and vines—and perhaps smaller plants. He may simply sell the

The garden is paved with gravel into which big flat stones are set. The fence is made of rough cedar boards and cedar saplings allowed to weather naturally. The plants were selected for interest, texture, color and general suitability to the garden, not because they are particularly Oriental in character.

Metamorphosis in a tiny city garden. The owner, who had lived in Japan, asked Stanley Underhill, Boston landscape architect, to turn the then rundown yard into a Japanese garden. This is the outlook from his dining room today. A small stream of water—just visible through the second window from right—tinkles into a minute pool made in a hollowed-out block of stone.

plants and let the homeowner plant them, or he may for an extra charge do the planting himself. Some nurserymen also operate a landscape contracting business which moves large plants, builds walls, puts in lawns, and does other such involved gardening jobs.

Nurserymen are good people to know because they are expert in growing, handling and caring for the major plants in the garden. Also, because they have usually been in business in the same community for a long time, they know which plants do well there and which do not. (None of this is true of the average garden-center operator.) But it must be stressed that while most nurserymen claim to be landscapers, they may not be any more skilled or knowledgeable than you are.

For real landscaping help you need to employ a landscape architect. He can be useful also for simple planting projects because he has considerable knowledge of plants (although he doesn't know as much about handling them as a nurseryman does). But his main proficiency is in garden design. This he has gained through his own innate sense of creativity and through four or more years of training in one of the universities offering degrees in landscape architecture.

This is the view of the garden as you enter it from the public walkway behind the property. The planting bed is raised behind the curb of logs. A redvein enkianthus conceals a curving section of sapling fence, which in turn conceals an air-conditioner.

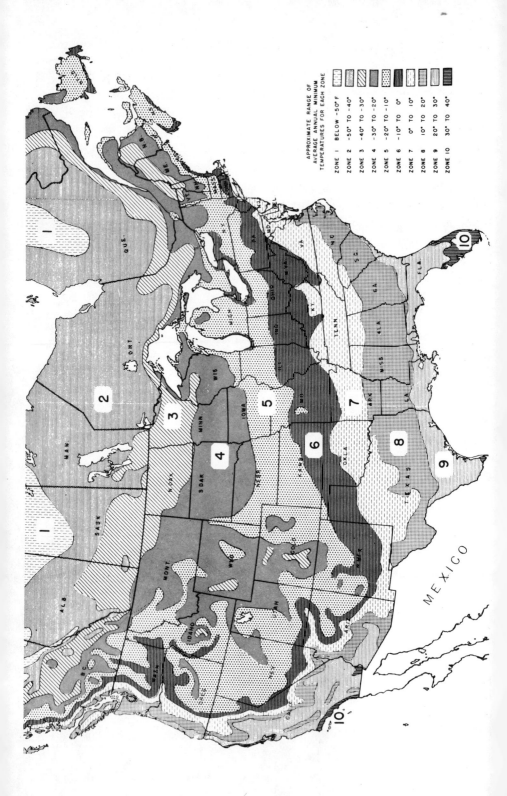

APPROXIMATE RANGE OF
AVERAGE ANNUAL MINIMUM
TEMPERATURES FOR EACH ZONE

ZONE 1   BELOW −50°F
ZONE 2   −50° TO −40°
ZONE 3   −40° TO −30°
ZONE 4   −30° TO −20°
ZONE 5   −20° TO −10°
ZONE 6   −10° TO 0°
ZONE 7   0° TO 10°
ZONE 8   10° TO 20°
ZONE 9   20° TO 30°
ZONE 10   30° TO 40°

Not all landscape architects are willing to undertake garden-remodeling projects. Many of the best known men and firms do large-scale civic and commercial work only. But the man who is currently the most famous in the profession is extremely active in the residential field, and there are hundreds of other excellent people like him.

All landscape architects work for a fee, the size of which depends on the fame of the architect and on how much work you ask him to do. If you want advice only, it's one thing; if he must draw a plan, it's another thing; and if you also want him to supervise the actual work on your garden, it's still another thing. Some men charge a flat sum for the entire job; others work on an hourly basis. In either case, of course, this adds to the total cost of your remodeling project. But if you want an outstanding garden, hiring a landscape architect is the best way to get it.

Plant Hardiness Zone Map developed by the Agricultural Research Service of the U.S. Department of Agriculture. On a more detailed version of the map, each zone is divided more or less in half into two sub-zones: "a" and "b." The former is farther north and somewhat colder than the latter.

2 Landscaping the Property

The definition of landscaping depends on who is giving it. To some homeowners (and practically all developers) a lot is landscaped if it has a grassy area that can be called a lawn and several shrubs around the foundations of the house. To others a landscaped lot doesn't necessarily have to resemble the gardens of Versailles, but it is one that has been developed and planted to create an attractive, functional setting for the beautification of the house and the enjoyment of the occupants.

I belong to the second school of thought. A lot cannot be said to be landscaped just because it has been tidied up and planted; it has to be tidied up and planted with a thought-out purpose. There's a difference, obviously—a difference of quality, though not necessarily of quantity.

To illustrate the point, Cary and Charlie—my No. 3 children—own a property that is only partially landscaped. The area that passes muster is a small section directly in front of the house. Though far from outstanding, it is planted pleasantly enough to make people coming up the front walk think, "This is a nice place." But the rest of the lot—to the sides and back of the house (a much larger area)—most definitely is not landscaped. It's neat and pleasant. There are a big lawn, several good trees and a number of flower beds and vegetable patches. But these just

This antique Vermont home was completely relandscaped by a flower fancier. The entire effect is of a simple unit, with all principal garden areas separated by plant borders or walks yet nicely interconnected to make for easy circulation.

Despite the imposing elegance of the house, the surrounding garden is extremely simple. The chairs indicate that this area is a place the owner finds restful.

happened. They have no rhyme or reason and serve no definable purpose except to provide open space.

On the other hand, you would have to say my No. 2 children's home is landscaped, because the things that were done were purposeful. But while the place is pleasing enough, the landscaping is poor. However, in comparison with Cary and Charlie, Randy and Bill are lucky, because they at least have something to build on when they start relandscaping.

Landscaping fundamentals. Landscaping is an art, just as architecture, painting and sculpture are arts. It is not easy, yet the fundamentals are readily grasped by anyone, and they are equally applicable to all properties regardless of size, shape, contours, surroundings and other variable factors.

1. The over-all purpose of landscaping today is to make a property functionally useful to its owner and, secondarily, to make it esthetically pleasing. This is not always understood, because in times past esthetics

A garden area specifically designed to be viewed from the living room and owner's bedroom. The lines of the sculpture, which sets the tone for the area, are repeated in the brick wall and carefully rounded Japanese hollies, one of which is off-centered in an encircling hedge.

were put ahead of function. The change has come about simply because we today spend so much more time outdoors; thus the land around a house has become a living space as important as the living space in the house.

2. In landscaping, the house and lot must be considered as one thing —a giant living space of which a small part happens to be under a roof. When developing the outdoor area, therefore, you must consider its effect on the indoor living area, and vice versa.

3. Despite the unity of house and lot, however, a property is divided by function into several small, rather well-defined spaces. The exact number depends on the needs of the owners, but there are five at most:

Indoor living area, which is the house itself.

Outdoor living area, which includes the terrace and any other spaces in which the family spends time.

Public area, which the public sees and enters.

Automobile area, which includes the driveway, interior (off-street) parking area, if any, and garage.

Work area, which is devoted to miscellaneous purposes, such as storing trash, drying clothes, storing tools (if they are not in the garage), penning up dogs, and so on.

4. To maintain some semblance of order on the property, these areas should be separated from one another—if not by definite barriers, such as walls and hedges, at least by psychological barriers, such as flower beds, edgings or abrupt changes in elevation.

5. All the areas, however, must be related like pieces of a jigsaw puzzle and interconnected so that you can move directly from one to the other. In landscapers' language this is called "good circulation," and it is essential to your use and enjoyment of your property.

6. Because few modern homeowners have the time, money or inclination to spend hours laboring over their properties, ease of maintenance is also essential. This is achieved not only by making it simple to move around the property as you work but also by arranging all areas and planting beds so they are easy to manage, putting in plants that require minimum attention, using paving where people walk (see Chapter 15), and so on.

7. From the esthetic standpoint the first requirement of successful landscaping is that it should suit the site and the house. Both the scale and style must be appropriate. You should avoid such things as Olympic-sized swimming pools on postage-stamp lots, Cotswolds-style flower beds surrounding contemporary houses, rock gardens on flat terrains.

8. Simplicity must be the keynote. Trickily shaped borders, jazzy paving, cute artificial fawns and silver gazing balls are as much out of place in a garden as power lines looping across the Rocky Mountains. Gardens are not meant to be theatrical settings. On the contrary, they should be restful; and restfulness is a product of simplicity.

9. The landscape design should complement the shape and contours of the lot, not emphasize its bad features. This is the same thing as buying clothes that bring out the best you have to offer. For example, if your lot is long and skinny, the principal lines of your landscape plan should be from sideline to sideline. If your lot is on a steep hillside, you

should plant it with low, spreading trees rather than tall species, which will accentuate the steepness.

10. The design should impart a sense of balance; otherwise you become uncomfortable in the garden. Balance does not require symmetry; a design can be asymmetrical and still balance. The important thing is that, viewing the garden, you should feel that the whole thing is in harmony—the right side doesn't overpower the left, or the planting in the background doesn't detract from that in the foreground.

11. If you have a view, the garden almost certainly should be oriented toward it. Lacking a view, you should create within the garden a focal point. Focal points, like views, create perspective and attract attention away from things that are unsightly or disturbing.

12. Finally, to be fully successful, the landscape design should enhance not only the view of the house as seen from the street but also views of the garden as seen from the house and from those places in the garden that you frequently occupy.

Developing a landscape plan: Step 1. As I said in the preceding chapter, the first step in remodeling your garden—which includes landscaping—is to take a good hard look at it to make certain that you are fully aware of its good features and bad. Study the following:

Lot lines
House
Driveway and garage
Terrain
Trees and large shrubs
Other important natural features
Neighboring properties
Street, sidewalk and street trees

And don't forget also to check local ordinances, deed restrictions and easements.

Step 2. Make a list of what you need and very much want on your property. Needs are, of course, more important than wants, so use some sort of mark to differentiate them. The list will include such things as these:

Terrace

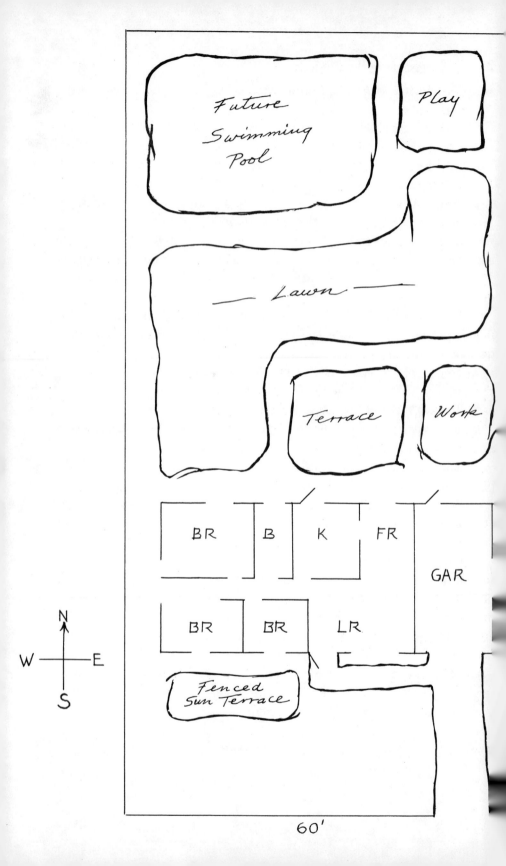

Off-street parking space for three cars
Dog pen
Play yard for children—big enough for jungle gym
Flower bed for cutting
Small vegetable garden
Future swimming pool

Step 3. Make an accurate sketch of your property. If you have a plot plan prepared by an architect or builder, use that. Or ask your mortgage company or the local assessor for help. If the plans given you are small, redraw them on graph paper to a scale of ⅛ or 1/16 inch to 1 foot. The ⅛ scale is best if your lot doesn't exceed 200 feet in length or width; use the 1/16 for a larger lot.

After establishing the lot lines, draw in the plan of the house, including the exterior doors and windows you most often look out of, the detached garage and driveway, and other buildings.

Then draw in all the trees and big shrubs you want to save. Indicate the trunks with X's, and sketch in the edges of the leafy crowns so you can tell how much of the ground they shade.

Finally, mark in the position of important, immovable features, such as streams, large rocks, telephone poles, and so on.

When the plan is finished, examine it carefully to make sure it's complete and accurate in every detail.

Step 4. You're now ready to start drawing a new plan. Here are two "don't's" that will help you: Don't rush. Don't despair if you seem to take forever to get anywhere.

Buy a large roll or pad of tracing paper and draw your plans on this so you don't mess up the basic plan of the property as it is now. Just place a sheet of tracing paper over the basic plan and go to work roughing in the principal spaces of the garden-to-be—the terrace, main lawn area, and so on. Don't try to draw the shapes accurately. All that is necessary is to establish the best positions for the spaces.

Once this is done, begin refining the plan. Work out the shapes and

OPPOSITE

The first step in making a landscaping plan is to draw an exact plan of the house and lot. Then start roughing in the outdoor spaces you want so you can see how they fit into the lot and how well they work together.

sizes of the garden spaces first. Then fill in with walks, trees and other major details.

One of the secrets in landscape planning is not to try to save tracing paper, because if you keep making erasures on a plan, it may become hopelessly confused. The best procedure is to draw a plan on one sheet, then draw a second plan on another sheet, and so on until you finally arrive at one you think perfect. In this way you avoid the confusion of erasures and gain the advantage of being able to compare one plan with another.

Another secret of good planning is to study each plan as if you were standing right in the middle of it. This is not as difficult as it may sound. If you can't do it with your eyes open, close them and imagine yourself looking out of the living room window at the terrace, then looking from the terrace across the lawn, then looking from the end of the lawn back toward the house, and so on. Only in this way can a person who is not trained as a landscape architect get a good visual picture of a landscape plan.

Step 5. Although you may be tempted to skip this step once you have settled on a landscape plan, don't do it. There is no other way for the average person to make certain that his plan is actually as good as it looks on paper.

The procedure is easy and also a lot of fun. All you have to do is stake out the important areas and features of the plan on the lot. Use a 50- or 100-foot tape and measure accurately. All the stakes should be of the same size and should be driven into the ground to the same depth so one will not appear more important than the others. To outline spaces, such as a terrace or play yard, stretch clean white twine between the stakes.

When the plan is completely laid out, step into it and take a leisurely stroll. Can you move around easily? Is there plenty of space to relax,

OPPOSITE

A finished landscape plan developed for an existing property by Frances Ely Zahm, landscape architect of Delray Beach, Fla., and Buffalo, N.Y.

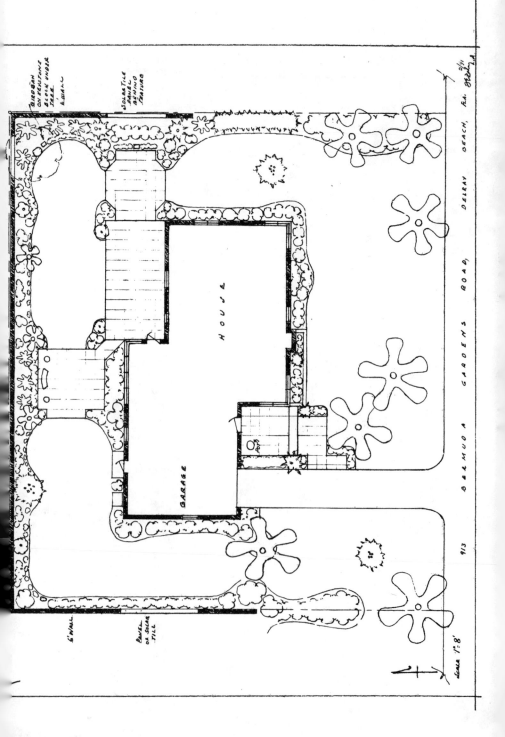

Southern and northern examples of excellent foundation planting. In both cases the plants are sufficiently varied to provide interest without giving a jumbled effect, and they are low enough not to block the windows.

play and pursue your favorite activities? Do you have shade and sun where you want them? Is the planting attractive?

If the answers are yes, it's time to roll up your sleeves and translate the plan into reality.

Changing foundation planting. If this isn't the hardest job in relandscaping a property, it is usually one of the most essential, because so many old houses have such miserable foundation borders. But before you start to replan them, make certain you understand what foundation planting is all about:

1. The purpose of foundation planting varies. It may be:

to conceal ugly foundation walls.

to conceal basement bulkheads, electric meters and other excrescences that mar the appearance of the house.

to make very tall, narrow houses look lower.

to frame very long, low houses and thus make them appear more compact.

to relieve the stark appearance of large, windowless wall areas.

to accent doorways and other desirable features of the house.

to provide a border between the house and lawn so you can mow without hand-clipping the grass, which would otherwise grow tall and straggly against the house.

2. The depth and shape of a foundation border is determined by the plan of the house, the width of the overhanging roof (because if a house doesn't have gutters, the water, snow and ice cascading from the roof may damage plants that are directly under the eaves), the plants you put into the border, the purpose of the border, and the landscaping of the surrounding area.

In other words, a foundation border need not be a straight bed exactly 3–4 feet deep (as most such borders are planned). On the contrary, it can range from 1 to 6 or 8 or even 10 feet deep. It can be curving or scalloped. It can project straight out from the house in a peninsula if the purpose is to conceal, say, a bulkhead or flight of ugly steps. It can extend well beyond the ends of the house to make it look lower. And so forth.

3. A foundation border is not meant to screen the windows of the

house. If screening is required, the trees and shrubs used for the purpose should be set out far enough so they will not cut off light and air in the house.

4. The plants in the border should not be arranged in a straight, neatly spaced row unless th re to be maintained as a hedge. Neither should they be arranged ᵢ.. a high-low-high-low roller-coaster pattern.

5. The height of the plans in the border is dictated by their placement. Ground covers and very low-growing shrubs are used only for the purpose of separating the lawn from the house. Slightly taller shrubs are used under windows. Tall shrubs and trees—usually columnar in shape —are used by doorways, at the corners of the house and to break the monotony of blank walls.

6. The selection of plants should not necessarily be limited to evergreens. Deciduous plants often serve equally well.

7. To avoid a jumbled effect, the plants used in any one border should be limited to three or four varieties that are used over and over again—but not in strict alternation.

The big problem in remodeling the foundation borders at the front, back and sides of an existing house is to apply these "rules" without ripping out everything you now own and starting fresh. Frankly, there is no simple solution, any more than there is a simple solution to relandscaping an entire lot that is already planted. The easiest course to follow is to leave the best of the existing plants where they are, discarding the rest and replacing them with something more suitable. The best course is to draw a plan for the borders as you would like them to be, throw out the poor plants, move the others to better locations as necessary and fill in the gaps with new plants.

3 Improving Soil and Drainage

If the plants in your garden are not growing well, it's a pretty positive sign that the soil isn't very good. Even if the plants don't show signs of malnutrition, soil deficiencies may be preventing them from being as thrifty as they should be.

Soils that are naturally good are not common in the United States. Most need some improvement. And in a great many gardens the soil needs very extensive improvement (1) because it is extremely sandy, gravelly, rocky or heavy with dense clay; (2) because all but one or two inches of the topsoil has been stripped off and sold by the builder; (3) because the lot has been filled with "unclean" fill; or (4) because the water table lies within a few inches of the soil surface.

How far should you go in making improvements? Since soil improvement is not inexpensive, it doesn't make sense to go further than is necessary to make it plantable. Confine your efforts to the shrubbery border, lawn or whatever area you intend to remodel. On the other hand, if the entire lot has impossible soil, a major overhaul is indicated.

Just recently, for example, I was talking with a family that had made the mistake of buying a house that, they soon discovered, was built on a quagmire. The septic field overflowed constantly. And rain turned almost the entire place into a pond.

This is a classic example of shysterism by developers and stupidity by town building authorities. The dangers of the situation are obvious, but what is not so obvious is the fact that if the family in question should ever want to redevelop the property, they could do so only by putting in a lot-sized drainage system and by persuading the derelict town government to provide a sewer to carry the water away.

Equally drastic steps are necessary when a developer leaves the buyer with a legacy of one inch of topsoil over a bed of gravel or rocky subsoil. In this case the only possible solution is to buy topsoil by the truckload to spread over the lot.

The A, B, C's of garden soil. Regardless of the size of the area that requires soil improvement and regardless of the types of plants you intend to put in, the soil should have certain general characteristics.

1. It must be adequately drained. That's because there are very, very few plants that can stay alive in waterlogged ground.

2. On the other hand, the soil must be capable of retaining some moisture, because there aren't many plants that will grow in dry sand or gravel.

3. The soil must have adequate depth for plants to put down their roots. The importance of this requirement is easily understood when you look at a lawn that is underlain here and there with large boulders. In hot, dry weather the grass over the boulders turns brown, because the roots can't go deep enough to get moisture, yet the surrounding areas remain bright green.

4. The soil must be porous enough for oxygen, water and plant roots to penetrate easily. Dense clay may be rich in all the nutrients that plants need, but it will not sustain plant growth unless it is broken up enough, first for the roots to take hold, then for water and oxygen to nourish them.

5. The soil must be reasonably fertile. That is, it must contain ample amounts of nitrogen, phosphorus and potassium—the principal plant nutrients—as well as small amounts of such micronutrients as copper, zinc and magnesium.

How to drain soil. The family I have just mentioned is in serious trouble. So are their neighbors. They live in a landlocked swale from which the impounded rain, snow and sewage water drains only when it gets so deep that it overflows the rim. Their only hope is to go to the town health authorities (because of the hazard created by overflowing septic systems) and raise such a hullabaloo that the town itself will take the necessary steps to drain the area or will force the builder to do so.

This, however, is a fairly unusual problem. Most garden drainage problems are no one's fault. Rather they are a fluke of nature, compounded sometimes by encroaching civilization. Nevertheless coping with them often requires considerable ingenuity.

1. Unfortunately, the classic solution to garden drainage problems is applicable mainly to rather large properties that are strategically located above a nearby stream, river or pond.

Dig trenches through the soggy area; place perforated composition drainpipes in the bottom; and lead the collected water away through a line of solid drainpipe to the nearby watercourse or, sometimes, a storm sewer. The manner in which the drains are arranged depends on the size and shape of the wet area. Generally the simplest pattern is fishbone-shaped. There is a straight central drain with branches flaring away on both sides. The space between branches should be about 6 feet.

The depth at which the pipes are laid ranges from 9–12 inches in a lawn area to 12–15 inches in flower beds and vegetable gardens to 18–24 inches in areas planted to shrubs and trees.

2. If the ground does not slope from the wet spot toward a convenient disposal area, you can dig a large, deep dry well in the center of the spot. For improved collection of water, install four or five drain pipes that radiate out from the well like spokes of a wheel for about 6 feet. Then install in the bottom of the well an automatic sump pump that lifts the water into the city storm sewer or natural disposal area.

Sump pumps are not too expensive yet are effective. I bought a portable unit several years ago that is capable of lifting 34 gallons per minute to a height of 10 feet. With it I can empty my 30,000-gallon swimming pool in less than a day. The cost was $70.

3. An alternative to removing water from the soggy area is to raise plants out of the water. This is done by digging out some of the soil in the area, building it into a mound and setting the plants on top. In flower and vegetable gardens the plants may be planted on parallel

ridges separated by ditches. But a more attractive solution—applicable also to shrubs and small trees—is to build raised beds surrounded by retaining walls of brick, stone, concrete blocks or redwood or cypress timbers. For more about raised beds see Chapter 7.

4. The simplest way to protect plants from excess water is to excavate the area to a depth of several feet and toss in a 6-inch layer of crushed rock or coarse gravel. However, this produces the desired results only if you have an occasionally high water table; and even then it may not be reliable if the soil is heavy clay. At my last home I lost a number of trees and shrubs that were planted in this way simply because the surrounding soil was so dense that, despite the layer of rock, the planting holes quickly filled with water that couldn't escape.

The other obvious drawback of this approach is that it is feasible only for small areas. To excavate to a depth of 2 or 3 feet over a large area would require too much work.

How to provide deep root room. I'm not talking here about providing adequate topsoil; we'll get to that later. This is a question of what you should do if your property is underlain with close-to-the-surface rock or hardpan.*

In some cases, where the impervious layer forms an unbroken sheet less than 1 foot below the soil surface, the only way you can hope to have trees and large shrubs is to blast out holes for them with dynamite and jackhammers. If the layer is within 6 inches of the surface, holes must also be dug out for much smaller plants, including grass, because they will quickly burn out in dry weather unless you water them heavily every day. On the other hand, if the soil depth exceeds 1 foot, most shrubs will survive; and in 2 feet of soil many trees will also come through (though you will have to stake them until they have had ample time to send out roots far to the sides).

Individual large rocks or outcrops lying close to the surface are much less troublesome, because you can usually plant around their edges instead of directly over them. Many can also be dug out by a bulldozer or even by hand. I have a friend who used to amuse himself on week-

* Extremely dense, hard clay. In the Southwest, where such clay is often mixed with salts, it is called caleche.

ends by coaxing huge boulders out of his lawn even when they defied his crowbar. His method was to find a seam in the boulder, douse it with water, turn a flamethrower on it for five or ten minutes while adding more and more water, and then give the rock a few heavy whacks with a sledge. Sometimes the treatment had to be repeated, but eventually most of the rocks broke into smaller pieces that could be easily handled.

How to make soil more moisture-retentive. Fast-draining soils are a problem, not only because water passes down through them before it can be absorbed by plant roots but also because nutrients are quickly washed down out of reach of the roots. The problem, however, is rather easy to correct by adding absorbent materials to the soil.

Humus is the favorite additive because of its ready availability and many desirable characteristics. But for maximum water-holding effect, clay is better.

When using humus, try to add about 1 part to every 3 or 4 parts soil. If this is too rich for your pocketbook, however, don't despair; even 1 part to 100 helps. On the other hand, I have found that if you exceed 1-to-3 proportions, the humus seems to speed the drying-out of the soil until it breaks down into tiny particles which fill the interstices between the grains of sand.

Clay can be used in somewhat greater quantities because it sops up and retains moisture better than humus. But it adds less nourishment to the soil and is harder to mix in.

How to make heavy soil more porous. The porosity of clay and other dense soils is improved by adding ingredients that separate the clay particles from each other. Most people rely on coarse sand, but better results are achieved by mixing small crushed rock, like that used on driveways, with the sand in equal proportions. An alternative is to substitute chopped tree bark or wood chips for the rock. This accomplishes the immediate purpose of breaking up the soil and also adds to the fertility of the soil as the wood decays. (Of course, there's no reason why you shouldn't use all three materials, not just two.)

How to increase soil depth. Nothing is more disheartening for homeowners than the discovery that there is almost no topsoil in their yard and garden. Even people who are totally lacking in gardening knowledge or experience can tell from looking at the soil their spade turns up when it is incapable of nourishing anything except weeds.

But don't give up hope. There are several ways to correct matters.

The easiest—and most expensive—is to buy enough topsoil to give you a total depth of 5 to 6 inches. To figure how much you need, determine the square footage of the area needing treatment. Then if you want to add 6 inches of topsoil, divide the answer by 2; for 4 inches of topsoil divide by 3; for 3 inches divide by 4; for 2 inches divide by 6. The result is your topsoil requirement in cubic feet. Divide this number by 27 to find how many cubic yards you should order. (Example: If you want to add 6 inches of topsoil to a 600-square-foot area, you need 300 cubic feet, or a little more than 11 cubic yards.)

People who sell topsoil advertise it either as just plain "topsoil" or as "screened topsoil." Generally one is as nutritive as the other, but the screened soil is the more expensive because it is free of rocks, roots, sods and other large rubble. Thus it saves you a lot of work, because you can plant in it immediately. If you buy ordinary topsoil, you should toss it through a coarse wire screen before using it; or rake and rerake it thoroughly after spreading to remove the undesirable matter. Either procedure is tedious and tiring and may result in considerable loss of material.

Another way to acquire topsoil is to scrape it from one part of the garden and pile it up in another. This is practical, however, only if you don't intend to plant the denuded area and are planning, for example, to convert it into a paved parking space or use it for a swimming pool or terrace. Some people who are eager to reduce garden maintenance simply cover the denuded area with gravel or crushed rock, but unless great skill is used to blend this into the landscape, the effect is likely to be disastrous. Offhand I can think of two properties that were partially covered with gravel in order to cut lawn work, and both look awful—like gravel patches.

A third way to acquire topsoil is by cover-cropping. This is a farming practice that consists of planting a quick-growing crop of rye grass, vetch or soybeans, plowing it under after it's about a foot tall, and repeating the process time and again until the soil is filled with humus. Results are equally good on a residential property, but for anyone who is eager to whip his garden into shape, they take much too long to achieve. The only place where homeowners ordinarily plant cover crops is in the vegetable garden.

How to improve filled land. About a year ago my dentist noticed that part of his hillside lawn was suddenly and inexplicably subsiding at an alarming rate. When one of his children happened to run across the area, his feet broke through the surface. With all manner of fearful thoughts passing through his head, the dentist got out his spade, dug down and discovered an enormous mass of rotting tree trunks and limbs that evidently had been buried by the builder of the house.

As the dentist's experience indicates, land that has been filled is not always easy to identify. But generally it is—especially if the property is close to a swamp or has a steep bank across one side.

Improvement must be undertaken before you try to plant anything, because the odds are that the area is so crammed with tree stumps, boulders and gravel that nothing will grow. However, since wholesale removal of the undesirable stuff is almost impossible, you are usually limited to digging it out only in holes for individual trees and shrubs. Make the holes as big as possible, and to compensate for the miserable surrounding soil (if you can call it that), refill with pure topsoil and humus. Elsewhere in the garden ignore the fill and cover it with as much topsoil as you can afford.

How to improve soil fertility. In recent years organic gardeners have made such a to-do about mixing organic matter* into the soil that you might think this is the only way to increase fertility. Let's get the matter straight.

Organic matter *is* the most important ingredient in soil. No question about that. So if you have to make your garden soil more fertile, the first thing you should do is to mix in ample quantities of peat moss, leaf mold, wood chips, chopped bark, grass clippings, pine needles, rotting hay, manure or decomposed matter from your garbage can.

But organic matter does not contribute everything your soil may need

* Decayed vegetable and animal matter—also called humus.

to support vigorous growth. And if you're in a hurry for plants to grow large and lush, organic matter by itself will not provide the answer.

The best way to increase the fertility of your soil is to go about it scientifically.

1. First test your soil. It's the only way to find out exactly what it is like and what you should do to make it better.

Soil testing can be done at any time of the year but is best done in the early spring or late fall. With a sharp, clean spade take thin, uniform slices of soil from ten to twelve places throughout the area needing improvement. If the area is to be planted with grass, flowers or vegetables, take the sample from the upper 6 inches of soil. In areas with trees and shrubs, take the samples from the upper 8–10 inches of soil.

Toss the samples together in a clean pail and mix them thoroughly. (If they are too wet to mix, let them dry out.) Then put about 8 ounces of soil in a plastic bag or other container and send it to your state agricultural extension service with a request that they analyze the soil and give you recommendations for improving it. Your letter should include (1) your name and address; (2) the size of the area you aim to improve; (3) what is planted in the area at the moment (you need not be specific—just say trees, vegetables, grass, or whatever the case may be); (4) what you intend to plant in the area (don't be specific about this either); and (5) a brief description of any very unusual features of the area (for example, it is heavily shaded by pines, a stream runs through the middle, or other special characteristics exist).

The addresses of the 51 state agricultural extension services are given in the Appendix. All make soil tests. Some charge nothing for the service, others ask 50 cents to $2. The test results should be returned to you within a few days or weeks, and will resemble the analysis illustrated on the opposite page.

2. One of the things a soil test is designed to determine is whether your soil is acid, neutral or alkaline. This is expressed in pH. If the pH is 7, the soil is neutral; if below 7, it is acid; if above 7, it is alkaline. Most plants grow well in soils having a pH of 6–7.2. If the pH is

OPPOSITE

A soil-test report on the author's vegetable garden. A report for a flower border, shrubbery planting or lawn would be similar, although the recommendations at the end of the report would probably be somewhat different.

FERTILITY OF YOUR SOIL

The Connecticut
AGRICULTURAL EXPERIMENT STATION -
P. O. BOX 1106   123 HUNTINGTON STREET   NEW HAVEN, CONNECTICUT 06504

FERTILITY OF YOUR SOIL ASSAYED BY THE MORGAN METHOD, A PRODUCT OF RESEARCH AT THIS STATION

The accompanying "Soil Testing" folder explains the symbols used below and contains other information helpful in understanding this report. If you took samples as suggested in "Soil Testing," the treatments suggested should be helpful on the areas sampled.

QUESTIONS on this report should be addressed to: SOILS. Box 1106, New Haven, Connecticut 06504

Mr. Stanley Schuler
Blood Street
Lyme, CT 06371

Date __March 27, 1974__

RESULTS OF TESTS - (RED D-DEFICIENT; d-PROBABLY DEFICIENT; e-PROBABLY EXCESSIVE; E-EXCESSIVE)

LABORATORY NUMBER	931				
YOUR SAMPLE					
CROP TO BE GROWN	vegetables				
SOIL TEXTURE	FSL				
ORGANIC MATTER CONTENT	M				
pH	5.40				
NITRATE NITROGEN	VL				
AMMONIA NITROGEN	ML				
PHOSPHORUS	L				
POTASSIUM	L				
CALCIUM	ML				
MAGNESIUM	M				
ALUMINUM	M				
MANGANESE	ML				
SUGGESTED TREATMENTS (IN POUNDS PER 1,000 SQUARE FEET)					
LIMESTONE	70 lbs.				
SUPERPHOSPHATE 0 - 20 - 0					
FERTILIZER GRADE	30 lbs. 10-10-10				

REMARKS: If a new seedbed, work lime in first (if indicated), then apply fertilizer and rake in, finally seed. If an established lawn, apply fertilizer when grass is dry.

below 6, however, the soil should be "sweetened" by the addition of ground limestone or hydrated lime. One is as good as the other. However, the former has a more lasting effect, while the latter works faster.

The amount of lime you should add will be noted in the soil-test report. If it exceeds 5 pounds but is no more than 10 pounds per 100 square feet, apply it in two equal doses six weeks apart. But if the amount of lime called for exceeds 10 pounds, apply it in 5-pound doses at six-week intervals.

3. If the plants you intend to put in are rhododendrons, azaleas, camellias, blueberries or other acid lovers, and if your soil has a pH of 6 or higher, steps must be taken to make the soil more acid. This can be done with finely ground sulfur, but the easiest way is simply to cover the ground around each plant with a mulch of oak leaves (best) or pine needles (second best). As these decay, work them lightly into the soil (but be careful not to hurt the plant roots) and add a fresh layer of leaves.

4. The final step in making soil more fertile is to add humus and fertilizer.

As indicated earlier, organic gardeners use humus alone, and there is no reason why you shouldn't also. Add as much as you like, but unless the soil is clay, don't exceed a proportion of 1 part humus to 3 parts soil.

Even with humus, however, your soil will be greatly benefited by the addition of a balanced fertilizer. Here again your soil-test report may make recommendations. If not, you must make your own selection between the many inorganic and organic powdered fertilizers on the market.

For most purposes I like the inorganic fertilizers, because they are generally less expensive and contain a higher percentage of chemical nutrients. For trees, shrubs (but not all), vines, ground covers and flowers, a 10-10-10 or 10-6-4 fertilizer gives excellent results in almost all parts of the country. But the fertilizer favored for lawns has a very high percentage of nitrogen: for example, 18-6-9 or 24-9-5.*

---

* The chemical formula of every fertilizer is printed on its bag in the form of three hyphenated numbers. The first number indicates the percentage of nitrogen in the mixture; the second the percentage of phosphorus; the third the percentage of potassium. The total of the three numbers is the actual amount of nutrients in the bag. Thus a 100-pound bag of 10-10-10 fertilizer contains 30 pounds of nutrients; the rest of the weight is made up of inert filler.

Organic fertilizers are generally rich in one element and contain only small amounts of the other two. Their main value is that they release nutrients to plants over a much longer period of time than the majority of inorganic fertilizers. Bone meal, dried blood and dried manure are three of the most widely used organic fertilizers. Cottonseed meal is particularly recommended for acid-loving plants such as rhododendrons and camellias.

Improving soil for a lawn. Topsoil for a lawn should be at least 4 inches deep. The subsoil should be porous and free of boulders, which will prevent the grass from putting down deep roots.

If the lawn area is not properly graded, strip off the topsoil. Pile it at one side and bring the subsoil to the desired grade. Spread the topsoil over this in an even layer and add humus, fertilizer and lime (if needed) on top. Then mix all the ingredients together with a rotary tiller and rake smooth.

Improving soil for trees and shrubs. Dig a hole for each plant. It should be half again as deep as the root ball of the tree or shrub and twice as wide at both top and bottom. Place the sods in one pile, the topsoil in a second, the subsoil in a third.

When filling the hole, toss the sods in first, then the topsoil. Mix the latter with 1 part humus to 2 parts soil, and add lime as called for. Finish filling to the top with the subsoil, which should also be mixed with humus and lime.

If the soil is dense clay, place a layer of crushed rock in the bottom of the hole and install a drainpipe leading away to a disposal area.

Don't fertilize a tree or shrub until it has been in the ground three or four weeks; then just scatter the fertilizer on the surface and scratch it in. The delay allows the roots to start functioning so they can take in the nourishment.

Improving soil in foundation borders. The foundation borders are normally planted with shrubs and small trees, so the preparation of the soil is similar to that just described. But an additional step should be taken to make up for the habit that builders have of tossing all manner of debris into the ground around the foundations of houses.

Generally such debris—consisting of wood, paper, concrete rubble, nails, glass, electric cable, plaster and plasterboard—is not harmful to plants. But a concentration of concrete can interfere with root development, and cellulose material not only attracts termites but also tends to deplete the nitrogen supply and causes the soil to subside when it decays. Consequently, when you dig planting holes, take pains to remove all the foreign matter you encounter.

Improving soil in flower beds. For annuals, perennials and bulbs, dig each bed to a depth of 12 inches; remove rocks and tree roots, and invert the soil so the topsoil is at the bottom and the subsoil on top. Then add humus, sand, crushed rock, lime and fertilizer as necessary and mix them in thoroughly with a spading fork or rotary tiller.

When the work is completed, tramp through the bed to pack it down and let the soil settle for a couple of weeks before planting. At the end of that time, if the level of the bed is higher than that of the surrounding ground, remove some of the soil so that what is left will not drift out of the bed when there's a heavy rain.

4 Removing Trees, Shrubs and Vines

One of the most determined and successful gardeners I know is a woman who defied neighborhood complaints by completely ripping out and redoing the garden of an old home that stood on the most prominent corner in her village. A year ago, when I was taking pictures for the third or fourth time of the beautiful place, I commented on the fact that a big tree at a corner of the driveway had disappeared.

"It was a pest," the lady said. "Nothing would grow under it. It ruined the lawn in that area. It just didn't do anything for the place, so I took it out and put in a smaller tree—a dogwood tree—instead. Now I'm about to get someone to take out those three swamp maples along the driveway and back of the garage."

"They're pretty big to give up," I ventured. They were a good 60 to 70 feet high.

"But they're a nuisance," she answered. "Dirty. Not very pretty. And they cut off too much sun. I love trees, hate to take them down. But there's no place for swamp maples on a small property."

The woman's attitude is exceptional. For most gardeners, cutting down a tree, shrub or vine is unthinkable. I find it difficult myself.

When we bought our house, the front walk was bordered on either side by a large yew hedge. "It's got to go," Elizabeth ordered, and I agreed. It was much too heavy-looking for the entrance, and it couldn't be cut back satisfactorily. But I found all sorts of reasons for not getting

The entrance of the author's home before and after the removal of large yew hedges bordering the short front walk. With the plants gone, the entrance has gained its rightful importance. The foundation planting to left of the door was also replaced. ("After" photo by Richard Beatty)

at the job, and they all boiled down to the fact that I just didn't want to give up anything that big, that handsome, that old.

The truth is, however, that unless a tree, shrub or vine is especially beautiful or has sentimental or historic value, there is little excuse for not taking it down or moving it if it is in any way a detriment.

Why plants deserve the ax. The greatest troublemakers are the trees, shrubs and vines that are planted close to the house:

They make the interior dark and even dank. This has always been an excellent reason for cutting them down, but it's especially so during the energy crisis, because (1) they deprive you of the warmth of the sun, and (2) they make the house so gloomy that you must burn electric lights during the day.

They precipitate the growth of mildew and algae on the house siding by restricting air circulation, shading out the sun and trapping moisture.

They stimulate the growth of moss on the roofs they shade and speed decay of wood shingles and shakes.

They smash holes through roofs when boughs are broken by storms.

They clog gutters and thus cause snowmelt running off the roof to form ice dams, back up under the roofing and come down through the walls and ceilings inside.

Vines clinging to masonry walls weaken the mortar and cause leaks.

But plants growing at a distance from a house may also need to be taken out:

because they continually litter the ground with leaves, twigs, branches and fruits.

because the roots invade and clog septic fields and house drains.

because the plants outgrow and crowd the garden.

Why not move instead of cut? Of course it isn't always necessary to take the ax to a plant that's getting in the way. But moving may not be a simple or practical alternative.

A vine is one thing. It makes no difference how big it is, it can almost always be cut back to the roots, dug up (the root system is not terribly extensive) and replanted. And because of the nature of vines, one that is replanted will usually put out stems and grow vigorously again.

But trees and shrubs are another matter. Some are too big to handle even by nurserymen with bulldozers and cranes. Relatively few can be cut to the ground with the assured expectation that they will put up desirable new growth. But the main problem is that, if they have been growing in a crowded location, they will be so lopsided that they are of little or no value anywhere else.

The yews I took out were a good example. The two at the front ends of the hedge rows were transplantable because they were solidly leafed out on three sides. So I moved them to new positions where the fourth side, which was black and needleless, could be placed against a wall. But all the other plants were worthless because they had been so squeezed together in the rows that they were devoid of needles on two opposite sides and were shaped more like sandwiches than well-rounded plants.

Don't, in other words, get your hopes up about saving big plants that are causing trouble. But don't, on the other hand, give up on the idea until you've read Chapter 5.

How to chop down a tree. Felling trees becomes progressively trickier as the trees get taller. There's an element of risk in every operation simply because you must use sharp tools. But there comes a point when the danger is so great that you should back off and hire a tree surgeon.

I wish I could be more precise about when that point is reached. If the tree you're taking down is in an open area, you can handle it with the proper tools, because it will do no damage wherever it falls. But if a tree is surrounded by plants you want to save or is close to the house, it must be small enough so you can bring it down without doing serious damage on every side. To be arbitrary, let's say it shouldn't be more than 30 feet high if you're working by yourself, 40 feet if you have an able-bodied assistant.

Trees can be taken down at any time of year, but the ideal time is in the winter when the ground is frozen hard and is immune to damage from falling limbs and trunks. Winter is also the ideal time to take down a tree that you intend to replace with a smaller plant, because then you have just a short wait for the spring planting season to roll around.

To fell a tree, notch it on the side toward which you want it to fall, then saw through from the opposite side just above the bottom of the notch. The notch, in this case, was cut out entirely with an ax.

The first step in tackling a tree growing in a restricted location is to lop off as many of the branches as possible. This permits you to drop it more accurately, because you are not fighting against the weight and pull of the longer or heavier branches. You can bring it down in a smaller space. And it gives you more freedom to cut the trunk.

If you're agile and the tree is big enough, climb as far up as possible and remove the branches from the top down. Use a coarse-toothed pruning saw; it is much safer to wield than an ax. If you can't climb the tree, remove all the branches you can reach from the ground, then put up a ladder and remove those higher up.

After taking off the branches, remove them from around the base of the tree so they won't trip you up as you proceed with your work.

If a tree is too tall to fall in the space available for it, or if the top is so crooked or lopsided that it's likely to pull the tree down where you don't want it to go, you have little choice but to top it before felling it. Get someone to help you, and do the job before you take off the branches below. Tie a rope around the top and have your helper, standing on the ground, pull slightly on the other end to guide the top down. Then saw off the top so it falls away from you—not down over your head. Topping a tree is generally inadvisable, because it's an awkward and rather dangerous business that you should undertake only if you have no alternative.

Whether or not you top a tree, it is a sound idea to rope the entire tree down to the ground so it won't smash into other plants or get hung up in nearby trees or wires. Tie the rope as high up in the tree as possible, and make sure your helper backs off beyond the tree tip when it's on the ground. The rope must be strong, sound and long enough to span from treetop to helper. (For example, if a tree is 30 feet tall, your helper should stand back from the base about 40 feet—which means that the rope should be at least 50 feet long.)

The procedure followed in cutting down a tree is to make a notch facing the direction in which you want the tree to fall, and then to make a cut from the opposite side of the trunk into the back of the notch. The notch, in other words, is the key to successful felling. But its position is not dictated solely by the direction in which *you* want the tree to fall. You should also consider how the *tree* wants to fall.

If the tree is straight up and down, it will go in almost any direction once lopsided branches have been removed. But if it's leaning or bent, its natural tendency is to fall as it is inclined; and it is difficult for you to persuade it otherwise. In fact, I wouldn't try except on trees that are small enough to be manhandled.

Once you've decided on which side to notch the tree, you must decide how high off the ground to cut the notch. The natural temptation is to make it just above ground level so you won't be bothered with removal of the stump later on. But since this means you must work on your knees and will probably end up cutting the trunk at an angle, it is much better to cut the trunk a foot or two aboveground.

Cut the bottom of the notch first. Use a pruning saw, hold it level, and cut to about the center of the trunk. Then with an ax, notch the trunk at about a 60-degree angle to the back of the saw cut. Check once more to make sure the notch is squarely facing the direction in which the tree should fall. If it isn't, deepen it on one side with your saw and ax.

Then saw through the back of the trunk into the notch. The cut should be about 2 inches above the bottom of the notch. As you get close to the notch, keep a wary eye on the top of the tree to see how it's leaning. If it's not headed in the desired direction, tell your helper— who up to this point has simply been keeping the rope taut—to put more strain on the rope.

Finally, when the tree begins to creak and bend, warn your helper, and stand back a little farther from the trunk as you continue sawing. Be careful not to stand directly behind the trunk, because sometimes, as a tree comes down, the wood suddenly gives way and the trunk kicks backward.

When the tree is on the ground, chop it loose from the stump and cut it into lengths for hauling away. Then saw the stump off at ground level.

How to remove stumps. Removal of stumps is essential only if they (together with their roots) are so big that they create a gap in the garden or if they start to grow again. The latter problem is rather common among deciduous trees, especially those that were young and healthy. Instead of being killed by cutting, they send up sprouts from the trunk or roots, and in no time these develop into brand-new trees. (Needled evergreens, on the other hand, almost always die when cut.)

Whatever the reason for removing a stump, the process is usually fairly easy if the root system is small. All you need is a shovel, crowbar, mattock and plenty of energy. But don't tackle big trees and shrubs. There are only two ways to cope with them.

One is to hire a tree surgeon to remove the trunk with a chipper. This is a costly operation, but if you want fast results, it's your only choice, especially if you're dealing with a really big tree.

The slow, cheap alternative is to kill the stump with one of the stump-killing chemicals on the market, and then burn it out. This you can do

If you want to stop a stump from sprouting but don't have to remove it (as described in the text), make a series of ax cuts all the way around the sides and fill them with Ammate, a powerful weed and brush killer.

yourself. Bore two or three one-inch or larger holes in the top of the stump to a depth of about 10 inches. Then bore several slanting holes through the sides of the stump until they intersect (hopefully) the vertical holes. Fill all the holes about two-thirds full of chemical and wet it with water. Then add chemical to the top of the holes, and cover the stump with plastic.

About a year later the stump and roots will have dried and decayed sufficiently so you can burn them out after dousing them with kerosene.

How to remove shrubs and vines. Simply because of their size, shrubs and vines are easier to handle than trees. But they can fool you too. A year ago, when I ripped out a row of old forsythias, I didn't anticipate any trouble, because these are brittle plants which had never before given me trouble. But this particular group turned out to be about as cantankerous as any shrubs I have ever dealt with. In fact, several were so obstinate that I had to leave the roots in place and hope that a potent dose of stump-killer would in time dispose of them.

Despite such experiences, however, I'd still rather remove a shrub or vine than a tree.

Start by cutting off the top to within a couple of feet of the ground. Then dig the soil away from around the roots. Chop through whatever roots you encounter with a spade, pruning shears or mattock. Then drive a crowbar in under the root ball, place a rock or short log under the bar as close to the end as possible, and pry away. If you're lucky, the plant will lift out of the ground like a baby's tooth. Some plants, however, will defy all efforts; in which case, you will have to cut the stems all the way to the ground, and then gradually chop the roots into chunks small enough for the crowbar to handle. The alternative is to tie a chain or heavy rope around the plant and yank it out with a tractor. But don't try substituting an automobile for a tractor.

5 Moving Plants

I'd much rather move plants than cut them down, and as long as they are small enough and have ornamental value or the potential of ornamental value, that's what I always do. True, there are some plants I don't keep, simply because I don't like or need the varieties; but among my children or friends I can usually find someone who can make good use of them. That's part of the pleasure of gardening—sharing what you have with others, and vice versa.

Moving plants is not a difficult job until you run up against a big one. Then the only thing you can do is call in a professional and hope that he has the equipment and know-how to succeed where you couldn't even begin to fail. It's amazing what big plants an experienced nurseryman can handle. Even so, a lot depends on the plant and where it's growing.

My favorite nurseryman is Eddie Miezejeski. He works almost entirely by himself, and owns nothing more than a small front-end loader. Yet he's moved plants that most people wouldn't dream of tackling. Just last year he moved an old apple tree with a 12-inch trunk from an orchard into a neighbor's garden. But when I asked him some time later if he could move a much smaller holly for me, he turned me down cold. Why? Because the holly was planted against a wall, which would prevent him from digging all the way around it; and it was so dense, wide and spiny that it would have been torture to handle.

But don't draw any conclusions from what Eddie did and didn't do. If you have a big tree or shrub you want to move but can't handle yourself, ask a local nurseryman whether he can do it for you. His opinion will cost nothing, and he may be able to save you a lot of money by salvaging a plant you couldn't reproduce in ten or twenty years.

When to move plants. The only people I know who like to move plants in the fall are nurserymen, and they do so mainly because it helps to extend their very short business season. This is not meant to imply that they are taking a grave risk, but the chances of success are not as good as they are in the spring, when plants are starting to make growth and have all summer to become established.

In other words, unless you have a compelling reason for moving plants in the fall, wait until the ground begins to warm up in early spring. Then work fast, because the plants must be shifted into their new locations before they start to leaf out.

Is the plant worth moving? Any good variety of plant is worth saving if there's a chance that it will develop into a healthy, reasonably well-shaped specimen. So don't be hasty about tossing out shrubs and vines just because they are misshapen or spindly. The odds are that with careful pruning and feeding, you can give them a new lease on life.

But trees are a question mark, because most of them are supposed to have a single, straight trunk, and if this trunk happens to have died back or been broken or permanently bent, a tree will not develop as it should. This is not to say that it may not turn into a very picturesque specimen; some of the most interesting trees are badly gnarled or asymmetrical. But by and large, a properly shaped tree is more useful and effective in the average garden.

Needled evergreens, both trees and shrubs, are even more of a problem, but for an entirely different reason. If all the needles on a branch die, the entire branch dies, and no new branch will come forth to replace it. This is why firs, hemlocks, pines, arborvitaes and similar plants that have been growing in confined locations are rarely worth saving. When you dig them up and get them out into the open, you discover that they have large black holes in the sides which will never show a sign of green growth.

Root pruning. The purpose of root-pruning a woody plant that you intend to move is to reduce the root system to smaller, more manageable size and at the same time to reinvigorate the system by forcing it to put out new roots. Thus the plant becomes better able to withstand the shock of transplanting.

Root pruning is done in the spring one year before the plant is moved. Use a sharp spade and thrust it straight down into the ground as far as it will go in a circle around the plant. The diameter of the circle for a plant with a stem or stems less than 1 inch across should be approximately 15 inches. Increase the diameter 8–12 inches for each additional 1 inch thickness of stem. To stimulate root development, fertilize the plant three weeks after the pruning has been done.

Despite its value, I must admit that I have never done root pruning, and I have never regretted my inaction. But my good luck is undoubtedly attributable to the fact that the plants I have moved were either fairly compact or had not been in the ground so many years that they had had a chance to develop a widespread root system. For instance, I have moved many an azalea and mountain laurel because, although the plants were quite old, these species tend to have rather small, well-defined root balls that are easy to dig up pretty much intact. And two years ago I moved a well-filled-out 9-foot white pine without root-pruning, because I had planted it (in the wrong place) only two years earlier and it still had the compact root system that came with it from the nursery.

But there's a pair of European birches in the corners of my vegetable garden that I wouldn't dream of moving without root-pruning. Five years ago, when I bought the trees, they were only 10–12 feet high and had root balls no more than 15 or 18 inches across. But today the trees are up to 20 feet, the trunks have more than doubled in caliber to 5 inches, and the roots run far to the sides. So if I wanted to move them (which I don't), I'd have to prune back the roots to a circle at least 3 feet across, and give the trees a year to develop new roots within the circle before I moved them.

How to move trees, shrubs and vines. One of the benefits of root-pruning plants a year before moving is that, when you do transplant them, you do not lose many of the roots—just a few small ones that have grown out beyond the circle of cuts. Consequently there is no need to prune the top to compensate for the loss.

If you move plants without root pruning, however, you will almost inevitably chop off some of the roots as you dig up the plant; and you should counterbalance this loss by cutting back some of the extraneous growth and longer branches in the crown. The best time to do this— simply because it makes the plant a little smaller and lighter to handle— is just before you start digging around the roots. Don't cut too hard if your patient is a tree or shrub: you don't want to spoil the shape of the plant. A vine, however, must be cut back almost to the ground—not because it requires such drastic treatment to survive but simply to make it easier to handle.

Before unearthing a tree or shrub, tie the lower branches up around the trunk so they won't get in your way. If the ground isn't already damp, water the plant well a day before digging so the soil will stick together around the roots.

Use a sharp spade that won't mangle whatever roots you strike. Cut a circle all the way around the plant first, then trench out around it so you can get in under the roots.

The diameter of the circle you cut cannot be determined arbitrarily. Obviously it should not be so tight that you cut severely into the root ball; on the other hand, it must not be so large that you can't lift the plant. (A cubic foot of soil weighs approximately 80 pounds. This means that a root ball measuring 2 feet in diameter by 8 inches deep weighs 160 pounds, while a 3-foot root ball 1 foot deep weighs over 500 pounds.) The best way to figure the size of the circle is to scrape away the surface soil until you can see the roots and get a rough idea of their spread. Then drive your spade down carefully to get a "feel" of the root spread. If you hit some roots but not many large ones, you're on the right track.

After digging out around the plant, work your spade in under it at a depth of 12 inches for small plants, 15–18 inches for big ones. Cut the roots growing straight down and loosen the root ball so it can be lifted out of the hole or tipped over to one side.

Once you have completely loosened a small plant, slide a big piece of burlap underneath, wrap it all around the root ball and tie it around the stem, and then lift the plant from the hole. If the plant is large, tilt it to one side and smooth the burlap underneath, then tilt it back in the other direction so you can pull the burlap all the way through. Then tie the burlap around the stem and lift out the plant. If the plant is too heavy for one person to handle, however, don't tie the burlap. Instead, get a helper, and together grasp the four corners of the burlap and lift out the plant. Then use the burlap as a sled to pull the plant across the garden to its new location.

Prepare the new planting hole according to directions in Chapter 3, and fill the bottom with sods and topsoil mixed with humus. Tramp the soil down firmly so the plant won't sink when you set it in. The distance between the soil and ground level should equal the thickness of the root ball.

Set the plant in the center of the hole and make sure it is straight and facing in the right direction. Then fill in around it with any remaining

A picture sequence showing how to plant a shrub, tree or vine, whether it comes from a nursery or is transplanted from some other part of your own garden. 1. Dig a straight-sided hole to about twice the width of the root ball and half again its depth.

2. After the hole is dug, toss the sods taken out into the bottom. Then mix the topsoil from the hole with lots of humus and toss it back into the hole. Tamp it well until the hole is the same depth as the root ball of the plant.

3. Set the plant (in this case a leucothoe from a nursery) in the hole and make sure the top of the root ball is level with the surrounding soil. Turn the plant until the best side faces forward and straighten it.

4. Cut away the burlap around the roots and push the loose edges down into the hole. The burlap will rot quickly. Then fill in partway around the plant with soil mixed with humus and pour in water.

5. When the hole is completely filled with soil, build a collar of soil about 3 inches high around the edges of the hole and fill the saucer with water.

Cut away the cords binding the plant and trim off any broken branches. Fill the ucer with water every three days for the next couple of weeks.

topsoil followed by the subsoil mixed with humus. As you pour in the soil, tramp it down well.

When the soil surrounds the bottom two-thirds of the root ball, fill the hole the rest of the way with water and let it settle out of sight. Then add the rest of the soil up to ground level. It should not come up around the stem of the plant higher than the old soil line.

Build a 3- to 4-inch-high ridge of soil around the edges of the planting hole. Fill the saucer thus created with water, and refill it every three days for the next couple of weeks. After that you can let nature take its course, but it's a good idea to spread a mulch of peat moss, leaf mold or other organic material in the saucer to retain moisture.

Most trees and dense evergreen shrubs should be staked to hold them upright against wind and traffic. For small plants, one stake made of 1½-inch-diameter lumber is enough. Drive the stake down until it no longer wobbles. Leave a 2- or 3-inch space between it and the main plant stem. Then tie the two together with soft twine or strips of cloth. Tie the twine tightly around the stake but leave it fairly loose around the plant so it won't girdle the stem.

For somewhat larger plants, use two stakes, one on either side of the stem.

For the largest plants, use three steel guy wires fastened to heavy stakes driven into the ground around the tree. Loop the upper ends of the wires around the trunk 3–6 feet above the ground so that they form a 45-degree angle with the trunk and ground. To protect the bark, run the wires through short lengths of hose.

How to move perennials. This is a very easy job. Simply dig up the perennials in the early spring and replant them at the same depth at which they previously grew. Since most perennials develop into large clumps in a few years, they are usually divided into smaller sections at the time of moving. Species with small fibrous roots can be pulled apart with the fingers. On larger species you must use a knife, or simply chop the roots into pieces with a sharp spade. In either case, save and replant only the outer roots; the old inner sections have little vitality.

How to move hardy bulbs. Hardy bulbs are those left in the ground the year round. They include daffodils, tulips, lilies, crocuses and many others. You can dig them up, separate clumps that are too large, and replant them any time after they bloom and the foliage has died down completely. However, the sooner this is done after the foliage disappears the better.

6 Cutting Woody Plants Down to Size

Pruning is the kind way to take care of trees, shrubs and vines that have grown too big for your property. For one thing, it is much less work for the gardener than moving or removing plants. And as far as the plants are concerned, it does less damage than transplanting.

But pruning plants down to size is the solution to your problems only if the situation meets several tests.

1. Will the plant come through the operation without ill effects?

2. After pruning, will the plant look attractive and contribute as it should to your house and garden?

3. Will regular pruning be unnecessary in the future?

If you come up with yes answers to all three questions, pruning clearly gets the call over moving or cutting, and it still comes out ahead even if you have to qualify the yes answer to the third question. But if the answer to the third question is a definite no, or if it is only a qualified yes to Nos. 1 and 2, more drastic treatment is indicated.

Pruning trees. Reducing the size of overgrown trees by pruning is a maybe-yes-maybe-no proposition. All depends on the natural habits of the trees.

If a tree normally grows to considerable size, cutting it back to acceptable proportions once it has reached the point where you consider it too big is a lost cause. No matter how carefully you go about the work you simply cannot lop off the top and sides of a tree and expect it to be pretty. On the contrary, it looks as if it had been butchered. On deciduous species, major branches are shortened to ugly, blunt stubs that sprout silly tufts of twigs and leaves. Needled evergreens are splotched with bare, black spots that will never turn green again.

The only possible way to make a large tree smaller by pruning is to cut off all the lowest branches up to 10, 15 or even 20 feet above the ground. Of course this doesn't actually change tree size, but the tree gives the illusion of being smaller, because the area under it is opened up for use and so you can see through to the far side. Furthermore, if the tree is growing close to a house, removal of the branches eliminates the barrier that has been darkening the interior of the house and thus serves the same purpose as removal of the entire tree. Remember, however, that this kind of treatment is limited to slender species that have long, fairly straight trunks and compact crowns, with branches that do not droop very much—for example, pines, firs, birches and sweet gums. Spreading trees would still take up too much space, and those with short trunks would still block the view.

A tree that is naturally small is more amenable to pruning, because you don't have to take off very long lengths of branch to make a pronounced change in its size. This means that you can cut the branches where they join other branches or the trunk, and no ugly stubs are left.

Major pruning for the purpose of reducing the size of small trees should be done in the spring, but no harm is done by removing an occasional branch at any other time. If the trees bloom in early spring, wait until the blossoms drop before bringing out your cutting tools. All other trees should be pruned in late winter or early spring before growth starts.

The initial step in cutting back a tree is to study what needs to be done. First determine how much of the top should be removed; then, which branches should be trimmed and where. If the surgery required is minor, you're ready to go to work. But don't rush. When you're working in the top of a tree, it's difficult to locate the branches you intend to cut, and you sometimes remove the wrong ones. So climb down frequently and check what you're doing. And if you think your original plan should be changed, by all means change it.

If a tree requires hard pruning, your job is a little different. In these circumstances, most people are inclined to be more gentle than they need to be. Actually, with the exception of needled evergreens, the majority of trees tolerate surprisingly extensive pruning. Several years ago, for example, I lowered a big sweet cherry tree about 50 percent. I didn't limit my cutting just to small branches; in order to bring the tree down to manageable size I also had to sever several branches up to 6 inches in diameter. Yet despite this ruthless treatment, the tree showed no signs of suffering. If anything, it grew more vigorously.

I don't advocate that you follow my example, however. For one thing, some trees are not as healthy as the cherry and can't withstand the loss of so much wood and foliage. For another thing, drastic pruning almost always ruins the appearance of trees. Pruning in easy stages over a period of two or three years is a better approach. Cut back the worst of the overly long branches the first year, then the next worst, and the next, until the entire tree is down to the size and shape you seek. (This is a simpler procedure than cutting back all branches a third, then another third, and yet another third.)

How to remove a large tree limb. First make a cut partway through the bottom of the limb about a foot out from the trunk. Then cut all the way through the limb from the top several inches out beyond the first cut. Finally, trim off the stub close to the trunk. This method prevents a falling limb from stripping bark from the trunk, as it would if it were cut off at the base in the very beginning.

When cutting back a branch of a shrub or tree only partway, make the cut just above a side branch that is growing in the desired direction.

Once you've decided which branches to cut and how much, the actual pruning process is simple and basic.

Never bob a tree as you do a head of hair, because this results in an artificially smooth outline pockmarked with stubby growth. Take off a branch at a time. If you're removing an entire branch (a good practice on trees with a great many branches), cut it off at its base parallel with and as close as possible to the trunk or larger branch from which it arises. If you're cutting off just a few feet of branch, always cut just above a bud or side branch that is growing in the direction you want the branch to go. Make the cut at an angle of about 60 degrees to the branch and roughly parallel to the bud or side branch.

Always remove the water sprouts* growing from branches and trunk. They are unattractive and may impede the development of the primary

* Straight, slender, succulent growths. They are often called suckers, which they resemble; but strictly speaking, suckers grow only from the roots.

The straight, thin shoots arising from the branches and trunk are water sprouts. They should be cut out to keep the tree open.

branches. In addition, they grow so rapidly that they soon stick far out to the top and sides of the tree, destroying its outline.

Needled evergreens are handled like other trees but present two unique problems: (1) Branches that are cut off below the lowest green needles die, and no new branches appear to replace them. So if you want to save a branch that needs shortening, be sure to leave some green growths on it—the more the better. On the other hand, if you don't want to save the branch, cut it off at its base so that the surrounding branches can more easily fill in the hole it leaves. (2) When the leader* of a tree is removed, one of the branches just below it gradually curves

* The growing tip of a tree (or any other plant). The top of the trunk.

upward to take its place. During this process the tree grows wider instead of higher; but as soon as the branch is established as the leader, upward growth resumes at a merry pace. This physiological phenomenon complicates the pruning of needled evergreen trees and means that once you cut a tree back to size, you must prune the top and sides almost every year to maintain the status quo.

The final step in pruning deciduous and broadleaf evergreen trees is to coat all cuts more than 1 inch across with tree paint to keep out disease organisms. If sap oozes from the cuts, wait until the flow stops before painting. On needled evergreens painting is unnecessary because the sap soon forms a hard coating over all cuts.

Pruning shrubs. Shrubs are pruned on the same schedule as trees.

A splendid example of how to ruin a shrub by lopping off the branch ends. This minor atrocity was committed by a town highway crew clearing the road edges.

The black openings in this fine false cypress hedge resulted when the branches were cut back below the last green growths.

If you're dealing with a needled evergreen such as a juniper or yew, you can cut back the branches as far as you want so long as you don't remove all the green growth. Try to make the cuts inside the plant—behind the ends of the adjacent branches—so they won't show.

Deciduous and broadleaf evergreen shrubs can withstand more drastic treatment. In fact, if a plant has grown too large and perhaps straggly, removing the tops of the branches is a mistake, because it forces them to put out from the cut ends new growths which soon tower higher than the original branches.

The best way to make a shrub more compact is to cut the main stems at the ground. If you're in a hurry for results, you can remove all the stems at once. When fall rolls around, you will be amazed (and relieved) to find that the plants have made as much as 12 inches of sturdy new growth. But as with trees, I prefer to remove only about a third of the stems in any one year. This reduces the shock to the plants and doesn't create large gaps in the garden.

Pruning vines. I have yet to discover any good reason to worry about the method used to cut back a vine that has grown too large. All vines grow so vigorously that whatever you do—whether good or bad—is soon concealed by the new growth that develops when the weather warms up in the spring.

This means that if you want to cut off the top or sides of a vine as you do on a tree, or if you want to cut off all or some of the stems at the base as you do on a shrub, there's no reason why you shouldn't. Of course, if the vine has grown thin and unkempt with age, the latter course produces a more shapely, compact plant. On the other hand, if the vine has for some reason been reduced to one or two thick stems that put forth a thicket of new shoots, leaves and flowers every spring, it's much better to shorten the stems that grow too long than to remove them entirely.

Pruning hedges. How you reduce the size of an overgrown hedge depends not on whether the hedge is planted with shrubs or trees but on whether the plants are deciduous species, broadleaf evergreens or needled evergreens. The rules are simple.

Needled evergreens must not be cut back below the last green growth. Therein lies a problem if you have a tall hedge that has been allowed to grow too wide, because you cannot make the hedge narrow enough so you can cut the top from a ladder. The only solution is to hire a tree surgeon who owns a cherry picker that will permit him to swing up into the top and reach across it with his shears.

Deciduous and broadleafed evergreen hedges, on the other hand, can be pruned as much as you like. If they grow too wide, you can cut them back to a toothpick; if they grow too high, you can chop them off at any point—even right down at ground level.

Three points should be borne in mind in all hedge-pruning operations, however.

1. Whether the hedge is a new one you have just put in or an old one you have cut back hard and are starting over again, begin shaping and training as soon as it starts to make growth. If you wait until it reaches the desired height, you are likely to have trouble bringing it under control.

2. Always trim a hedge so that the sides slant in slightly toward the top or are vertical. This allows the sun to reach the branches at all levels. If a hedge is even slightly V-shaped, the lower branches sooner or later will die for lack of sunlight.

3. Take care not to let a hedge grow so wide that you cannot reach across and trim the top with a pair of shears. Hedges under 5 feet high should not be more than 6 feet wide. Those over 5 feet high should be no more than 3 feet wide if you can reach them from only one side, 5 feet if you can reach them from both sides.

7 Changing and Putting In Flower Beds

When spring comes, my No. 2 children—Randy and Bill—are going to come face-to-face with a problem they won't relish: something drastic must be done about the flower bed that came with their new old house.

It's a bed that would terrify more seasoned gardeners than they. Stretching about halfway across the back of their property, it is 8 feet deep, 60 feet long, and curves forward at both ends another 15 feet. It's jammed with perennials that haven't been divided in years. And to make matters worse, it is also jammed with rocks that the previous owner imported from afar so he could boast that he owned a rock garden (which has no place in that part of the country, which is flat and devoid of rocks).

"You've got to get rid of it," I said when I first saw it. And despite Randy's horror, I have stuck to my guns. If you're a confirmed gardener, with all the time in the world to devote to your garden, mammoth flower beds are a pleasure, not a chore. But for the average family they begin as a pain in the back (when you try to whip them into shape) and quickly develop into an even worse pain in the neck (when you give up the struggle and let them revert to a mess of weeds).

What to do with old flower beds. What you do with the existing flower beds in your garden really comes down to a question of "Do I want to raise flowers or not?" I love flowers, and I can't imagine not growing them even if I am reduced to caring for no more than one pot. But there are plenty of people who feel otherwise—some because flowers don't interest them in the slightest and others because they're physically unable to cope with flowers or simply don't have the time or inclination.

If you vote against raising flowers, the beds they have been growing in should be eliminated; otherwise they will turn into eyesores. The obvious things to do are either to plant them with shrubs or convert them to grass.

Shrubs are expensive but a good choice if the beds are next to the house or other building or adjacent to the lot lines. They might also be a good choice if the purpose of the beds is to divide the garden into areas—say, the lawn on the front side of a bed and a play yard at the back. Another advantage of planting shrubs is that they require the same kind of soil preparation as flowers and are most easily cared for in the same kind of beds.

On the other hand, putting old flower beds into grass makes sense if the beds are already surrounded by lawn, located where they interfere with mowing, or are so large that the cost of planting shrubs would be prohibitive. Grass, in other words, is cheap. But there are more problems in making a lawn out of a flower bed than meet the eye.

How to switch from flowers to shrubs. This requires fairly hard work but is a simple undertaking.

1. Dig the entire bed with a spade or spading fork and take out and discard (or give away) all flowers, bulbs and weeds. If the beds contain daffodils, tulips or day lilies, you must dig down at least 1 foot to make sure you eliminate all the bulbs and roots.

The slightly less arduous alternative to digging up a flower bed is to kill the vegetation in it with a soil fumigant such as Mylone or Vapam. These are extremely toxic chemicals, however, and must not be applied within 3 feet of edible plants or under the branches of trees and shrubs.

The best time to use a fumigant is when the soil temperature is 60 degrees or higher. First chop off the tops of all growing plants with a hoe and cultivate the soil to a depth of 6 inches or more. Apply the fumigant according to the directions on the package and water it in thoroughly. If the bed is small, covering it with sheets of plastic helps to increase the effectiveness of the chemical slightly, but is not essential. After two to four weeks, depending on the temperature of the soil, all vegetation, seeds, insects and fungi in the soil should be killed, and you can start planting the new shrubs.

2. Dig individual planting holes for the shrubs according to the directions in Chapter 3. If the flower bed was deeply dug, the soil in the bottom of the holes should be about as good as that near the top; and there is no need to reverse positions when refilling the holes. But to make sure that the shrub roots are well nourished, mix several spadesful of peat moss into the soil in the bottom of each hole.

3. After planting and watering the shrubs, cover the soil in the entire bed with a 3- or 4-inch-thick mulch of peat moss, chopped bark, buckwheat hulls or partially decomposed leaves. This will keep weeds from sprouting, hold moisture in the soil and help to nourish the shrubs as the mulch decomposes.

How to switch from flowers to grass. 1. Dig up or kill the flowers, bulbs and weeds. If you dig, it is not so important to remove deeply planted bulbs, because whatever growth they put up will be killed by mowing.

2. The worst problem encountered when a flower bed (or any other cultivated area) is converted to a lawn area is the settling of the soil which takes place for a couple of months after the seed is sown. However, this can be largely prevented if, after digging the bed to eliminate existing growth, you compact the soil with a heavy roller or by tramping through it, water it heavily, and let it settle for two or three weeks.

3. Add topsoil and humus (if necessary) to the bed and compact it with a roller until it is level with the surrounding ground.

4. Loosen the soil with a rotary tiller, three-pronged cultivator or hoe, rake it level, and sow grass seed. Follow the directions in Chapter 11.

If you intend to keep an old flower bed. Obviously I am not concerned here with keeping a flower bed you have had for many years.

Let's dwell instead on the family that buys a new home with a flower bed they know nothing about except that they want to keep it—for a while, at least.

The first problem such a family faces is the identification of the flowers in the bed. Why is this important? Because until you know what gold and fool's gold you own, you have no sound basis for deciding whether to keep the bed as is or replant it.

I ran into this problem when we bought our present house. There were two flower beds which we knew instantly we wanted to keep because they were well shaped and placed—just the right size for our needs. But it was November, and except for the iris, phlox and coralbells that grew here and there, I had no idea what the beds contained. I hoped for the best, however, because the previous owners, who had moved out three years earlier, were reputed to have been excellent gardeners. Why, I asked myself, go to the time and expense of ripping out a garden and discarding plants that might very well prove to be a delight?

When the flowers started coming up in the spring I was able to identify most of them. There were some bulbs and lots of perennials— all good, standard types that we liked. So I let the beds carry on through the summer. But they turned out to be disappointing.

With a few exceptions, the flowers were mediocre varieties. More than half of the phlox had reverted to the pallid purple of the original phlox. The tulips, which were scattered all over the place as if they had been dropped by birds, were garish. And both beds were so overgrown that I couldn't have squeezed in a single new plant.

Suffice to say that I dug up both beds; threw away almost everything, and started fresh the following spring.

Rash treatment? A foolish waste of time? I don't believe so. In the first place, the beds might have turned out as I had hoped; so if I had destroyed them without giving them a chance to show their colors, I would not only have deprived us of much beauty but would also have had to spend money needlessly on new plants. In the second place, I discovered a number of unwanted tulips and daffodils that I would not have known about had I dug up the beds immediately, because they were so deeply buried. True, if I had replaced the beds, the bulbs would have made their appearance anyway in among the new flowers; but they would have been hard to exhume without damaging the flowers. As it was, when I did dig up the beds, I had no trouble finding and getting rid of the bulbs. Finally, by waiting a year, I got a better idea of how badly overgrown some of the best plants were, and I was able to divide them to greater advantage than I would have otherwise.

Once you know the condition of an old flower bed, mark the plants you want to save with strong wood or plastic labels stuck deep into the ground beside them. Reconstruction of the bed can then proceed, whether in the fall, or better, in the early spring as soon as the soil begins to warm. The following steps should be taken:

1. Dig the entire bed to a depth of 1 foot and discard the useless plants. Label and set the others aside out of the sun. Cover them with wet burlap if you don't have time to divide them that day.

2. Spread humus to a depth of 1 inch or more over the bed. Add lime if necessary. It's also a good idea to add bone meal. Mix them thoroughly into the soil and level the bed.

3. Divide overgrown perennials into smaller sections. Save only the outer parts of the roots; discard the worn-out inner parts. Divide bulbs too. Then replant the bed and mark the location of the plants.

4. If you're reducing the size of the bed and converting it partly to grass, it's usually better to seed the grass after the flowers are planted, because in this way you have more freedom to move around and there is no chance of accidentally stepping into the grass-seeded area. If possible, separate the seeded area from the flowers by a permanent or temporary edging of boards, bricks or metal. Tamp the soil in the seeded area well and add new soil to bring it up to the level of the adjacent lawn. Then loosen the soil, sow seed, and roll the area.

How to build a new flower bed. Steps in preparing the soil for a new flower bed are covered in Chapter 3; but there is more to building a flower bed than that.

• Orientation to the sun. Depending on the genera,* flowers grow either in the sun or in the shade. There are also some that grow in

---

* "Genera" is the plural of "genus." A genus is a group of plants with basically similar characteristics. The genus is made up of different species; and some species are made up, in turn, of different varieties. When botanical nomenclature is used, the generic name comes first, the specific name second, and the varietal name last.

A border filled with phlox, astilbe and other colorful perennials faces down the south side of the old Vermont home pictured earlier. The tree is a white birch.

both, but they almost always have a preference. Because of this, it doesn't make a great deal of difference whether a flower bed is exposed to full sun; if it isn't, you can plant it accordingly.

By and large, however, the most brilliant flowers—the ones most people prefer—are sun lovers; consequently the usual advice to gardeners is to put flower beds in the sunniest spots available. A bed that is out in the open, well away from the house, trees, shrubs and other tall things is ideal. Only slightly less ideal is a bed built against the south wall of a house, fence or wall, or row of trees and shrubs that are not allowed to spread forward.

• Placement in the garden. If the purpose of a flower bed is to decorate the garden—not simply to serve as a source of cut flowers—you should obviously place it where it will be seen during the warm months, when you spend so much time outdoors. On the other hand, you obviously shouldn't just stick it anywhere you can enjoy it, because it may be in the way of family activities or look out of place. There are three rules for locating a flower bed:

1. It must have some visual or practical relationship to the immediate surroundings. In other words, it must be something; it must belong. For example, I don't think I have ever seen a flower bed in front of a wall which didn't look at home. The flowers help to soften the geometric lines of the wall and perhaps make it look lower and less formidable than it would otherwise appear. At the same time the wall serves as a background for the flowers, helps to accent their forms and bring out their colors.

On the other hand, a round flower bed in the middle of a lawn is almost invariably disturbing—ludicrous—because it's a misfit.

2. If you have an active family—especially if you have children—a flower bed should be out of the way. Place it next to the terrace, against the house, around the sides of the lot. But keep it out of the middle of the lawn, where children play.

If there are only adult or sedentary persons in the household, however, this rule isn't applicable.

3. Although the bed should be located where you can enjoy it in summer, try not to place it within direct view of the windows through which you normally look out on the world in winter. The reason for this

A combination shrub and flower border. Viburnums and small andromedas serve as the background for roses, snapdragons and blue salvia. The entire bed is mulched with chopped tree bark.

is that, except in our warmest climates, a flower bed in winter is not pretty; and it's a mistake to let it spoil the view from indoors.

• Shaping and sizing flower beds. A flower bed can be any shape you like as long as it fits into and contributes to its location. But the simpler it is, the better. For one thing, simple designs are always more pleasing than complex designs. They are much easier to work out; therefore they are less likely to have flaws. And they do not compete for attention with the flowers in the bed—and the flowers are, after all, the raison d'être of all flower beds.

The height of the flowers can be variable, but the depth of the bed should be limited so you can tend the flowers and cultivate the bed without stepping into it.

If the land is reasonably flat, the bed should be no more than 30 inches deep if you can get at it only from one side, 60 inches deep if you can get at it from both sides. If a bed slopes from front to back, it is usually accessible only from the low side, and its depth can be increased roughly 1 inch for each 4 degrees of slope. For example, a bed with a 20-degree slope can be about 35 inches deep; one with a 45-degree slope can be about 41 inches deep.

• Raised beds. A raised bed is one elevated above ground level by encircling walls of brick, concrete block, stone or wood timbers. It serves several purposes, although only one may be of importance to you.

On a steep slope it provides a level, erosion-proof place to raise flowers (as well as shrubs and ground covers).

Placed in front of a wall, it helps to relieve the blankness of the wall and makes it look lower, less imposing.

It gives elevation to a flat lot.

It protects the flowers from traffic, children playing, automobiles in the driveway, and other sources of possible destruction.

It keeps tree and grass roots from working their way into the bed, where they compete with the flowers for moisture and nutrients.

On property with a high water table it raises the flowers out of the water and keeps them from drowning.

It simplifies cultivation and management of the flower bed, since you don't have to stoop so much to work in it. In fact, you can sit down while you work.

A raised bed such as that at left protects the plants and makes them easier to care for. It also tends to make a wall or fence against which it is built appear lower and less forbidding. Raised beds are particularly valuable in cramped gardens.

In view of this rather imposing list of advantages, it is not surprising that raised beds have been fast increasing in popularity. But it's well to note some of the relatively minor disadvantages before you build a similar bed.

For one thing, a raised bed is harder to build and costs much more than an ordinary ground-level bed; and if you decide to get rid of it, that's a chore too.

Like anything that's raised above the garden floor, it is hazardous if you don't look where you're going when you are walking through the garden.

And it is much more difficult to fit into a garden esthetically than a conventional bed. In many gardens, indeed, it simply doesn't belong because of its artificiality.

Raised beds range in height from about 6 to 24 inches. I have seen them as high as 36 inches, but unless these are very shallow or planted to shrubs or ground covers, they are too hard to manage, because you need a stepladder to climb into them. The walls, of course, must be sturdy enough and extend far enough into the ground so that the pressure of the soil and accumulated moisture in the bed will not tip or topple them.

If a bed is built against the house, care must be taken to waterproof the foundation walls of the house to a point above the soil in the bed. (The soil must, of course, be several inches below the house framing or siding; otherwise the wood will soon be rotted out or eaten by termites.)

• Soil level. I doubt that anyone building a raised bed would be tempted to pile in soil higher than the surrounding walls, because it's obvious that it would soon wash out. But I have seen many ground-level beds in which the soil was higher—even a couple of inches higher—than the adjacent ground. From the standpoint of appearance this is not terribly objectionable. But it's almost impossible to keep the soil in the bed even if you dig a little ditch around the edges. Sooner or later the ditch fills and then the soil escapes, much in the way that molten lava rolls down from Hawaii's famed volcano Kilauea.

When you dig a new ground-level flower bed you should always compact the soil and let it settle for several weeks. Then, as a rule, you have to remove some of it in order to lower the level permanently about 1 inch below the adjacent lawn.

• Edgings. There's no necessity for edging a flower bed (or any other type of bed or border) if you're willing to keep the edges trimmed at all times and if you sharpen the lines every few weeks with a spade or steel edger. But a permanent edging saves a lot of work. How much depends on the kind of edging that is used.

Metal is not very good. The thin rolls of aluminum that are most commonly sold are, in fact, useless. They are almost impossible to install in a crisp line. They bend and twist if a baby steps on them. And they don't extend deeply enough into the ground to keep out grass roots.

Thick, rigid steel edging is far superior, but it has become almost impossible to buy. And like all thin edging materials, it makes for difficult mowing.

The ideal edging material is not sliver-thin, in other words. It should be thick enough—no less than about 1½ inches—to support one wheel of a mower. This makes it possible to edge the grass around a flower bed during normal mowing operations.* And there is little likelihood that the mower wheel will fall off the edging into the bed, causing you to damage the mower blade on the edging or to scalp the edge of the lawn.

The best edging materials are bricks, square-cut stones, thin concrete blocks, poured concrete and decay-resistant timbers. All materials should be at least 6 inches—and preferably 8 inches—wide so they can extend into the ground deeply enough to prevent twisting when stepped on. (If you are using bricks, be sure to set them on end to form what is known as a soldier course. Never lay them flat or on the long side.)

Laying out a flower bed. If a bed is accessible from only one side, place the lowest flowers in front and grade backward to the tallest. In a bed you can reach from both sides, the tallest flowers usually are placed in the middle and you grade down in both directions from them.

Generally flowers should be grouped in clumps of three to seven of the same variety. But occasionally they are used in long, ribbonlike drifts of about fifteen plants of the same variety. And in edgings they are used singly or in combinations of two or three varieties.

In laying out a bed, the clumps are placed like eggs in a basket or logs (as seen from the cut ends) in a pile. The drifts—if used—twine through these.

If you raise flowers from seeds, space the plants as recommended on the seed packets. But if you start with grown plants (as more and more homeowners are doing), follow these rule-of-thumb suggestions from my earlier book, *The Gardener's Basic Book of Flowers:*

Space flowers that grow no more than 6 inches high 6–8 inches apart.
Space flowers that grow 6–12 inches high, 8–10 inches apart.
Space flowers that grow more than 1 foot high 12–15 inches apart.

* Such an edging is also known as a mowing strip.

Space giant flowers, such as cosmos, tithonia and sunflower, 2–3 feet
   apart.
When flowers requiring different spacing are planted next to each other,
   divide each figure in half and add the answers. Example: If you plant
   a flower requiring 6 inches of space next to one requiring 12 inches,
   provide spacing of 3 inches plus 6 inches—9 inches.

Use the higher of the two figures given for each classification of plants
if your soil is of average quality and if you provide average care. The
lower spacings should be used only if you have good soil, if you keep the
plants very well watered at all times and if you fertilize them every four
to six weeks with a balanced inorganic plant food.

8 Improving the Contours of a Lot

Once a lot has been developed and built on, the land rarely is given a face-lifting. This is particularly true of small lots. But whether it's a small lot or large, the lack of attention is traceable to two things. (1) The owners are disinclined to have anything happen to the plants on the property. (The same feeling keeps them from cutting down trees or shrubs that darken the interior of the house.) (2) There often isn't space for earth-moving machines to maneuver.

The first argument doesn't impress me, but I have no comeback to the second. About twenty years ago I would have said, "Okay, if there's no space for a bulldozer, why can't you have the job done by hand?" But I learned my lesson in 1968 when we moved into our house and tried to locate our deep well, which for some odd reason had been completely covered over and "lost." I knew approximately where it was and figured it would be a simple job for a man to dig a 5-foot trench to it from the well house. But no such thing. Even in this rural area I could find no one who would dig a trench by hand. I had to get a man with a backhoe.

Despite this almost complete dependence on mechanical equipment, however, and despite the problems of using mechanical equipment on developed residential property, I don't see how I can omit this chapter. *You* may not read further, but some one else will. There must be hundreds of thousands of gardens that need remodeling not because they

To add interest to this lawn the owners scooped out the large center area and surrounded it on three sides with low banks sloping gently down from higher ground. A wading pool was built in the middle of the sunken area.

are overgrown or badly laid out but because the land is shaped unattractively or impractically.

When to regrade a garden. It's perfectly obvious that the best time to alter the contours of a lot is when it is sparsely planted. In other words, get at it—if you can—when it's new.

Another excellent time to regrade is when you build an in-ground swimming pool. This is an enormous job that not only requires large machines that wreak equally large damage but also affects a much greater area than is occupied by the pool itself. Furthermore, excavating for a pool produces a huge quantity of soil, which you may be able to use to fill in or build up other parts of the property.

Other construction projects—for instance, making an addition to the house or rebuilding a driveway—present similar opportunities for regrading, although they rarely have such far-reaching effects as the installation of a swimming pool.

However, if a garden requires regrading more than anything else, it's a mistake to wait and wait and wait for the ideal time to start the work. Just get at it—in early spring, when plants are dormant, and provided the excavating contractor takes pains to dig up the smaller plants so they can be replanted.

Cutting down high spots. Whether you need a bulldozer or just a pick and shovel, this is a very simple operation. The only point to remember is that the more soil you remove, the poorer the soil that remains. To compensate for this, dig the high spot 6–12 inches lower than the desired grade and refill with some of the topsoil you take out. If you don't have enough topsoil, mix it with subsoil and a bountiful helping of humus.

Terraced areas and low retaining walls give the illusion that this house is at a lower elevation than it would seem to be if the ground sloped steadily up to it from the street. Wintercreeper grows on part of the lower wall.

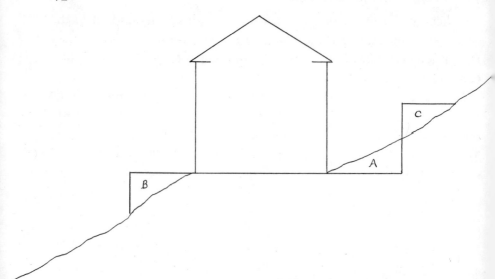

If you are making a terrace on the uphill side of a house, the soil excavated at A can most economically be used to create another level space at B or C.

'*Filling low spots.* If a good stand of grass carpeted the low spot, take it up in sods and use them to surface the spot when filled. (You should also do this when cutting down a high spot.) Work with a very sharp, flat, square-edged spade. Wet the grass first so the soil will stick together. To simplify relaying of the sods, divide the area lengthwise

To make a large flat area with minimum movement of soil, dig out at A and build up at B. The dotted area shows how much more earth you would have to move to make a flat space of equivalent size if you didn't build up at B.

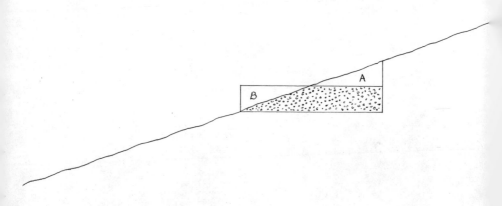

into strips of equal width. Stretch strings between stakes to mark the edges of the strips. Cut along the strings with the spade, and then cut the strips across into short lengths. For ease in handling, the sods should be about 1 foot square.

Lift each sod by slicing underneath it with your spade held as flat to the ground as possible. The sod should not be more than 1 inch thick, and can be a little less. Try to make all sods the same thickness. As they are removed, put them in stacks to one side of the low spot. Cover with damp burlap or canvas if you don't expect to relay them the same day.

When the sods have been dug up, scoop the topsoil out of the low spot and replace it with subsoil to within 7 inches of the ultimate grade level. Tamp well, and apply water if the soil is very dry or porous. Spread the topsoil into the excavation and tamp it into a 6-inch layer. Then loosen the surface with a rake, level carefully and set in the sods. Roll them firmly into the soil and water well. For further directions see Chapter 11.

Molding flat land to make it more interesting. This should be considered only if you live in an area where the land for miles around is as flat as a pancake. Then whatever you can do to relieve the monotony of your own property will add interest to your entire outlook. But if you own a flat lot that is surrounded by undulating land or hills, leave well enough alone; you can't improve what nature has provided.

Molding flat land to make it more interesting and attractive is primarily a job of changing the elevation. You can do this in several ways. (1) Build a low, spreading mound, plant a couple of trees, and pretend it's a grassy knoll in a meadow. (2) Create a large bank- or wall-rimmed sunken area in the center of the lawn. (3) Raise the terrace to the first-floor level of the house so that it is higher than the surrounding garden. (4) Shape the back lawn like the main floor of a theater—with a very slight slope down from the house, a reflecting pool in place of the orchestra pit, and a "stage" at the rear lot line.

Grading hillside lots. Although living on a hillside has certain advantages, it also has disadvantages that can make you forget how exciting it is to emulate an eagle. There isn't enough flat space on which

Retaining walls built of stone laid without mortar are more attractive than concrete walls but should be built by a professional if they are as high as this. (Photo by Warwick Anderson)

to walk around, play and relax. Climbing the hillside may be arduous. And going down may be dangerous.

Terracing a lot—dividing it into one or more flat benches that are supported at the downhill side by banks or walls—can correct both problems. How you do this depends on the natural contours of the lot, the placement of the house, how much flat space you need and for what purpose, the location of trees and large shrubs, the ease of excavating and filling the land, how next-door lots are terraced, and the problems of providing easy, safe passage up and down the hillside.

Since there are so many possible variables, some compromise is inevitable, and the "rules" I offer are nothing more than suggestions:

If possible, limit terracing to the areas that are naturally most nearly level. Thus there will be less earth to move.

Provide the largest flat spaces next to the house, where you need them not only for family enjoyment of the garden but also to protect against water running downhill into the house. In addition, a large flat space on the uphill side permits more light and air to enter the house.

Bear in mind that the deeper you make a terrace, the higher the banks or walls in front and back must be. Very high banks and walls are ugly, costly and hard to maintain.

Do not build terraces more than 5 feet high in front of the house; otherwise the flights of steps required to reach them will be tiring and

This low stone retaining wall is chockablock with small perennials planted in the chinks. Such an arrangement is called a wall garden.

dangerous. However, higher terraces are permissible—but not advisable —in other parts of the yard where there is less traffic.

Match your terraces as nearly as possible to your neighbors'. If you don't, you may have to build retaining walls between the properties.

To retard runoff of water, either make sure that a terrace that is planted to grass or other types of plants is perfectly flat or slope it backward slightly. A paved terrace, however, must be sloped backward to a drain or from the four sides toward a central drain.

To reduce the cost of terrace building, use the soil you take out to fill in immediately below the excavation or to build another terrace elsewhere on the lot. The drawings explain the reason for this commonsense practice.

Building banks. Whether to use banks or walls to hold up terraces is not always an easy question to answer. Both methods have good points and bad.

A bank is easier and cheaper to build, especially as the height increases. And because it's covered with plants, it blends better into the landscape, looks less artificial. But it takes up much more space than a wall and reduces terrace area accordingly. It is likely to erode, requires a great deal of maintenance, and if planted to shrubs, becomes cluttered with wind-blown debris. Finally, it may have a special fascination for children, who use it as a sliding board.

A wall is the exact opposite on every score, but people are much more likely to injure themselves if they stumble over the edge. On the other hand, while a wall does not blend into the landscape, it can serve as a delightful background for plants set in front of it.

In building a bank you must consider how it will be planted and what effect this will have on your gardening.

If a bank rises no more than 1 foot vertically for every 3 feet horizontally—that is, if it's sloped no more than 20 degrees—it is mowable, and there's no reason why you shouldn't cover it with grass. If the slope is more acute, however, mowing is impossible (except on a very low bank), and consequently you should cover the bank with a ground cover or spreading shrubs. On an extremely steep slope—for example, one that rises 1 foot vertically for each 1 foot horizontally—you must further reinforce the soil by sinking boulders into the bank between the plants. The alternative is to cover the bank with closely spaced horizontal railroad ties or logs that are held in place with stakes.

Building walls. Building a retaining wall to keep a terrace from sliding downhill is a much more exacting job than building a bank or ordinary wall, because the weight of the soil exerts so much pressure against it. I have seen many retaining walls that cracked from top to bottom because they were poorly designed or built. And I have also seen walls that toppled right over on their faces.

To avoid similar disasters you shouldn't try to build a retaining wall over 3 feet high yourself; and you shouldn't even attempt this height unless your soil is very well drained.

The wall can be built of stones, concrete blocks or poured concrete. If you use stones they should be as large and flat as possible to assure their fitting together tightly. Make the wall at least 2 feet thick, and slant it backward very slightly. It should be built up from a below-ground footing of rubble.

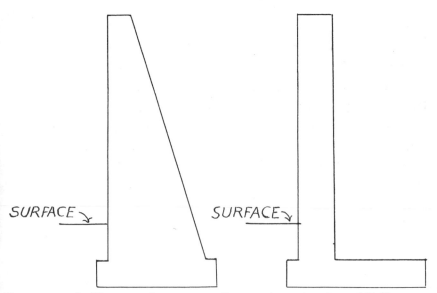

Two ways to build a poured concrete wall to retain an imaginary hillside or terrace at the right.

A concrete-block wall must be reinforced with half-inch steel rods spaced 2 feet apart. A poured concrete wall, on the other hand, does not require reinforcement but must be at least 8 inches thick. Both types of wall should be built up from poured concrete footings that are 16 inches wide and 8 inches high. The bottom of the footings should be at least 18 inches below ground level. To relieve water pressure behind the walls, make 3-inch weep holes at 10-foot intervals just above the ground level at the base of the wall.

Higher retaining walls should be built of poured concrete by professionals. Two types of wall recommended by construction engineers and masonry experts are illustrated. The L-shaped design is reinforced with steel. Both types should incorporate weep holes to allow moisture to escape.

Building a wall garden. A delightful way to change the level of gently sloping land is to build a wall garden. This is nothing more than a stone retaining wall—usually not more than 24–30 inches high—with plants inserted in the joints.

As with an ordinary retaining wall, start by digging a trench 6–12 inches deep and fill it with small stones, rubble, coarse gravel—anything solid. Pack it firmly. Then build up the wall with more or less rectangular rocks. It should be at least 2 feet thick and slanted backward 2 inches in every 1-foot rise. As you build the wall, fill in behind it with topsoil mixed rather heavily with small stones, and spread plenty of topsoil into the wall itself.

Set in little plants, such as basket of gold, sedum, creeping phlox and armeria, as the wall goes up. Don't plant them too thickly; leave about as much space between them as you would in a flower bed. Place the crowns of the plants slightly back from the face of the wall and spread the roots out on the soil between rocks. Mist with water and soak the soil behind the wall. When you reach the top, put in some plants on the wall and just behind it.

Raising the level of the ground around a tree. Probably the most common mistake homeowners make when they change the contours of their lots is to pile soil high up around the trunks of trees. If they don't

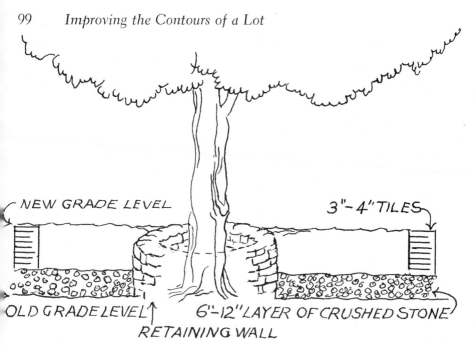

NEW GRADE LEVEL   3"–4" TILES

OLD GRADE LEVEL↑   6"–12" LAYER OF CRUSHED STONE
RETAINING WALL

How to raise the grade level around a tree.

know any better, of course, it's hard to blame them. But when friends on two recent occasions pointed to trees and asked, "Don't you think that will be all right? I know it's against the rules, but I tried not to pile up the soil higher than a foot or so," I had to rein myself in to keep from calling them blockheads.

Because one of the surest ways to kill a tree is to mound soil against the trunk and/or bury the roots deeper than they normally grow. So don't, don't. Ever.

If you want to save a tree, you must protect the lower trunk with a tree well. This is a concrete-block wall surrounding the trunk up to the new grade level. The inside diameter should be a minimum of 3 feet. Do not use mortar.

After the well is built, pour a 6–12-inch layer of coarse crushed rock over the ground from the well out to the tips of all branches, and cover it with an inch or two of fine rock. The purpose of this is to allow moisture and air to reach the tree roots and to keep soil from clogging the interstices between the rocks.

Finally, fill in around the well with soil, and cover the well opening with a steel grating to keep out children, animals and debris.

No additional work is necessary unless the depth of the fill and crushed rock exceeds 2 feet. In that case you should install a ring of 4-inch vertical drainpipes around the tree under the tips of the branches. The pipes should extend from the surface of the soil down to the original grade level. Space them about 4 feet apart, and cover the tops with wire mesh to prevent clogging.

Lowering the grade around a tree. While it's safe to raise the grade around a tree at any time, lowering the grade should be done only in the spring, to give the tree an opportunity to recover from the loss of roots that the process entails.

First dig a trench all the way around the tree at a point midway between the trunk and the branch tips. Carefully trim off the roots that are exposed. Then lay up a wall from the bottom of the trench to about 3 inches above the soil surface. This can be made of poured concrete or concrete blocks laid in mortar. You can also use bricks or stones, provided the wall is at least 8 inches thick and bonded with mortar.

Then dig away the soil outside the wall down to the new grade level. Mix fertilizer into the soil within the wall, and water it in well.

Building decks to provide flat space on a hillside lot. When one of my friends in California decided he needed more space for outdoor living, it didn't bother him in the least to discover that he couldn't possibly alter the contours of his hillside lot. He just built a couple of decks, and he's been happy ever since. Now his family has a comfortable place to relax in the shade of the trees that grow just uphill from the house. His children have a private, fenced-in play area that dries off quickly after it rains. He damaged or lost only a few of the shrubs and flowers he had planted. He was able to save a fine old eucalyptus that would surely have been cut down had he tried to terrace the lot. And he saved money.

Building decks is California's favorite way of making hard-to-grade hillside lots usable, and it's an equally good solution for problem lots in other parts of the country. In fact, many homeowners who have started out with a single deck that they use as a substitute for a conventional

In order to build a terrace below the level at which an old elm grew, a brick wall was built around the tree to enclose the upper roots.

patio wind up building a series of two or three or even four interconnected decks so they can relax and play on their lots wherever they like. (The decks may also serve as pleasant way stations for people toiling uphill to the house.)

Decks are harder to design than to build, because they are subjected to many stresses and strains; consequently they must be carefully engineered to assure that they will not collapse. However, if you select timbers of the proper size and tie them together securely with the recommended galvanized-steel fasteners, you should have few problems. For the technical information required, I refer you to either *The Complete Terrace Book*, which I recently wrote, or to the U.S. Forest Service Handbook No. 432, *Construction Guides for Exposed Wood Decks.**

The design of a deck depends on its size, height above the ground and the velocity of the winds to which it is subjected. Understandably, a

* Send $1 to the Superintendent of Documents, Washington, D.C.

high-level deck built on a steep slope must be more sturdily put together than a low-level deck on a slight slope. Both, however, are constructed in basically the same way of decay-resistant lumber.

At the very bottom of the structure are the footings and piers. The former are big, thick slabs of poured concrete which are placed in the ground below the frost line in cold climates, or at a depth of 2 feet in frost-free climates. The piers, which rest on the footings, are also made of concrete and are shaped like blunt pyramids. The tops project above ground at least 6 inches.

The piers support the posts that raise the deck to the desired level. These are usually made of 4-by-4-inch or 6-by-6-inch timbers, but are sometimes made of steel or reinforced poured concrete. To prevent lateral movement they must either be sunk into the piers or fastened to them with steel anchors.

Beams laid across the upper ends of the posts and attached with heavy steel flanges serve as the principal horizontal supports for the deck. They range in size from 4-by-6-inch timbers to 6-by-12.

The floor joists are installed at right angles to the beams. Made of 2-by-6s, 2-by-8s or 2-by-10s spaced 16 inches apart, they may rest directly on top of the beams, to which they are attached with spikes driven on the diagonal, or they may be hung against the sides of the beams in U-shaped steel hangers.

The floor of the deck is generally made of 2-inch-thick boards spaced one-quarter inch apart and nailed at right angles to the joists. If a tree is allowed to come up through the floor, a hole about twice the diameter of the trunk is provided to allow for an increase in trunk girth. An even larger hole is required in a very high deck so the tree will not batter the deck as it sways in a high wind.

If a deck is built as a free-standing structure and is over 5 feet high, it should be braced with timbers nailed diagonally from post to post. If a deck is attached to the house, however, bracing is not required, though it's advisable on very high decks. The connection between deck and house is made with a ledger strip. This is a 2-by-4-inch or 2-by-6-inch timber that is fastened to the house wall by spikes or lag bolts driven into the studs. The deck beams or joists are nailed to the top of the ledger strip or hung at its side.

Railings are required around the open sides of all decks, though they are often omitted on low-level decks. But you run a risk if you don't put them up, because it's just about as easy to break a bone falling 12 inches as 12 feet. For maximum security, let the posts supporting the deck extend above the floor and nail the rails to them. An adequate alternative is to bolt 2-by-3-inch uprights to the beams or joists under the outer edges of the deck and nail the rails to these.

On a low-level deck, if you want to obscure the railing, bolt 2-inch steel pipes to the beams or joists and thread stainless-steel wire of the type used for sailboat stays through them.

9 How to Use and Cope with Rocks and Outcrops

Several years ago, during a talk to one of the local garden clubs about gardens in winter, a small collective sigh welled up from the audience when I showed a picture of a large granite mass rising up in the middle of a lawn. It was an interesting, unexpected reaction. The photograph was not exceptional. Neither were the outcrop or setting. Pictures I had shown earlier of far more beautiful gardens and plants had elicited no such response. Why, then, did this particular shot appeal so much to the group?

It was simply because rocks in a natural setting have a beauty that is unlike anything else in nature. I feel this very strongly, yet I cannot adequately explain it. Rocks are nature's sculpture. They have color, texture and rare tactility. They are the ideal foil for trees, shrubs, grass, flowers and other plants. And most important of all, they impart a sense of solidity, to which we instinctively cling in a world that seems so full of instability.

Lucky is the homeowner who has a handsome boulder or outcrop in his garden.

Taking advantage of outcrops. Although any rock that shows through the surface of the ground is, properly speaking, an outcrop, the word is generally reserved for strata and boulders that are too enormous to move. There are four ways to cope with these.

One is to cover them up. My unscientific observation leads me to believe that this is the approach taken by new gardeners and those who come from a part of the country where outcrops and rocks are unknown. But as most of these people eventually realize, concealment is no solution to the problem.

Trying to cover an outcrop with soil and then putting in grass or other plants almost never works, because as soon as the weather turns dry, the shallow soil bakes out and the plants die. Training vines or rambler roses over an outcrop is easier and less costly, but while the shapeless mass of greenery may improve the appearance of a jumbled pile of small rocks, it merely detracts from the outcrop.

The second possible way to deal with an outcrop is to leave it alone and let nature take its course. The results are unpredictable.

If the outcrop is fairly smooth and uncracked, nothing happens. The rock may become encrusted with a few more lichens, but otherwise it looks the same after ten or twenty years as it did in the beginning. If the rock is cracked, rutted or generally uneven, on the other hand, plants take root in the thin soil that blows into the depressions. In some cases the effect is pleasant. A picture that never fails to appeal to viewers is that of a big tree growing out of a narrow crevice in a rock. But the effect more often is simply disheveled. And as time goes by, it gets worse, because, as the plants die, they crumble into humus, which adds to the supply of soil on top of the rock and encourages still more luxuriant growth. In fact, if the outcrop is porous and crumbly—like Hawaiian lava—the thriving plants ultimately break the entire rock down into a mound of soil.

If you like the appearance of an outcrop with plants growing in its seams, the best way to achieve it (the third way to cope with an outcrop) is to plant it yourself and to keep the plants under control after that. But this is doubtful business, because you must first find plants that will survive in very little soil. These include such evergreens as creeping junipers, periwinkle and English ivy. Sedum, creeping thyme and wallflowers are also possibilities, but they die down in winter.

The last solution to the problem is the best. Strip everything from the outcrop and let it stand out in all its rugged, timeless grandeur, without any competition except from the lichens that may encrust its surface

When this garden was remodeled ("overhauled" is a better word) the owner stripped all the vegetation from the large outcrops, which were almost everywhere, and then transplanted choice small shrubs to the fissures.

and from the plants in the garden surrounding. An additional benefit of this approach is that, once the rock is bare, it requires very little attention.

Removal of soil and vegetation is less arduous than you might think. First scrape off everything you can with a trowel and a knife. Sweep thoroughly. Then wash down the outcrop with a high-pressure stream from a hose. Collect the soil that's removed and use it elsewhere in the garden.

Taking advantage of boulders. Handsome as rocks are, there's a limit to how many you can use to advantage in a garden. A few choice specimens strategically located are much better than a plethora scattered

The owner of this garden, on the other hand, chose to remove all vegetation and soil from a huge ledge (foreground) and to leave it completely bare. The ground cover between the outcrop and terrace is pachysandra.

across the landscape. This is partly because the familiarity of a multitude breeds boredom—if not outright contempt—and partly because too many stones simply get in the way.

In a lawn, boulders are a nuisance, and the more you can get rid of the better. Those resting on top of the ground are the worst, because weeds growing under the edges are hard to control. But boulders that are buried to within a few inches of their tops are just about as bad, because they interfere with mowing and have no display value. The only ones worth saving—but only if they're too big to move—are those that stick up prominently and look as if they were part of an outcrop.

In among trees, shrubs, ground covers and flowers, boulders are of course less of a problem. Even so, it is possible to be too richly endowed, especially if the boulders have been piled into a heap by the glaciers or someone with a bulldozer. Consequently it's best to save the largest and most handsome and dispose of the others.

How you treat those you save is just as important as the removal of those you don't want. One of my more distant neighbors offers a prize example of what not to do. In clearing out the woods in front of his house he uncovered a boulder about half the size of a Volkswagen. Unfortunately, however, it wasn't any prettier than a Volkswagen, and he should have let shrubs and ferns grow back in around it to soften its lines. But he chose instead to turn it into a monument by building a circle of small stones around it. The next time I drive by I won't be surprised if there's a flag or maybe a gazing ball standing on top.

This is not to say that boulders bequeathed by nature should not be prominently displayed even though they lack great beauty. But unless they have extraordinary form, texture or color, they should not be featured like Venus de Milo. And under no circumstances should any attempt be made to adorn them except with planting such as nature herself would supply.

Adding stones to the garden. The fact that you don't live in New England or one of the other rocky parts of the United States is no reason why you shouldn't import stones and use them—one here and one there—for garden ornament. But don't make the mistake of trying to emulate the Japanese, because their feeling for stones and their facility with them is totally foreign to our ken. And don't think you're a garden-clubber making a flower arrangement, because few things turn out more disastrously than an arrangement of stones.

Some Americans may have an intuitive knack for using stones as garden ornaments, but most must learn by the trial-and-error process. To assist you, here are a few suggestions taken from my earlier book, *Gardening with Ease*.

1. Stones are made to order for those spots in the garden where lack of sun, poor soil, bad drainage and other such discouraging factors make it difficult to grow plants. Needless to say, however, you should not use them in such locations unless they improve the appearance of the areas and are, in turn, complemented by the areas.

2. Since stones weigh too much to permit you to experiment very much with their placement, one of the first things you should decide is whether to use a stone as a prominent feature (like a statue) or as a subtle element designed to surprise and delight the visitor. Stones that fall into the first category need to have plenty of space around them and should be set against a contrasting backdrop. (They are especially attractive when placed on an open paved or graveled surface. And they would be equally effective on grass—if you could figure out some way to avoid trimming the grass around them.)

Stones that play a subtle role in the garden can be tucked away almost anywhere, but should not be so hidden that visitors might trip over them.

3. Stones usually look attractive in front of walls made of brick, concrete block, vertical boards, and plywood, but not in front of shingled or clapboard walls.

4. Because they are natural objects, stones should be placed where you would find them in nature—on the ground. This does not mean that they must always be at your feet, of course. They can be at eye level, or even higher if they are on a hillside. But they should not be raised by artificial means. They should neither sit atop tree stumps or pedestals nor be placed in an obviously precarious position from which logic tells you that they would fall if some one had not indulged in a little trickery with mirrors.

5. It is important, too, that a stone be set in a vertical or horizontal

The interesting collection of light-gray stones that "sprout" more or less casually from this terraced hillside was gathered from all around the countryside.

position according to its placement in nature. For a slab of limestone to be set on end, for example, would not only be unnatural but would make it look like a tombstone. By the same token, it would be wrong to lay a spire of sandstone from a desert canyon flat.

6. The textured quality of a stone is enhanced when it is in sunlight

Here a massive, pockmarked pudding stone was brought in and placed in the shrubbery planting just behind the little statue. It's a good example of how to use a stone for ornament without making it a bold feature.

or light shadow. It suffers when it is in mottled sun and shade. And in deep shade it looks like nothing at all.

7. Some types of stone are great collectors of lichens, which add immeasurably to their beauty. The conglomerate rocks found in the Shawangunk Mountains of New York State, for example, are noted for their coverings of these strange little plants. If you can find handsome samples of similar lichen-covered stones, grab them quickly. If you can't, look for stones with a rather rough surface and place them in an exposed part of the garden where they will be struck by the winds that carry lichens across the country.

10 New Plants for Old

I have discussed long enough the difficulties of forcing oneself to tear out and discard healthy plants simply because they happen to be in the wrong place or are of an inferior variety. But I must say again that if you want to give new life and beauty to an old garden, this is one of the things that must be done.

In this chapter, however, I am not just talking about removing a plant and leaving a hole in the garden. That's hard to do but not nearly as hard as ripping out a plant and replacing it with something better—because that costs money! Nevertheless, having done it a good many times, I can assure you that once you've recovered from the shock to your pocketbook, you will be as delighted as you are when you trade in your trusty old car for a brand-spanking-new one.

There are a great many trees, shrubs and vines that do not merit space in any garden, let alone a garden that its owners want to be good. These include sumacs, poplars, ailanthus, swamp maples, catalpas, mulberries, many willows, black locusts, bittersweet, old weeping forsythias, many mock oranges, wild cherries, sassafras, sycamores, gray birches, many honeysuckles, kerrias, and so on. If you cannot identify the inferior plants in your garden by name, you undoubtedly know which they are through observation and experience. These are the plants you should remove and replace with something a great deal better.

The lists that follow give you a wide selection of outstanding plants

Why should anyone tear out *perfectly good plants* and replace them with something else? Here's one good reason. In this case the view of the swimming pool (not the wading pool in the foreground) from the house was blocked by an overgrown border of forsythias. And the house and

lawn were invisible from the pool. The only way to correct the problem was to rip out the forsythias and replace them with a pair of deep red rhododendrons and four pink azaleas. As a pleasant by-product after the change, a fine stone wall that had been almost buried in the shrubbery was brought to light.

ABOVE AND OPPOSITE
Here a border filled with ratty forsythias and mock oranges—none of which bloomed well in the shade of pines and firs—was replaced with a few smaller, shade-tolerant plants.

from which to choose. Many are well known and widely used; others are rather rare but available if you will take the time to ferret out a source of supply. A local nurseryman can be a big help here, because even though he may not carry the plants you want, he knows the wholesale sources that carry them.

An important point to note is that all the plants described below grow best in full or almost full sun. Outstanding plants that grow in shade are described in Chapter 12.

Selected Trees for Sunny Areas

ACACIA, SILVER WATTLE. *Acacia decurrens dealbata.* Zones 9–10. Broad-leaf evergreen. 50 feet. Fast-growing but short-lived tree, blanketed in winter with clusters of fragrant yellow flowers. Small leaflets give the entire tree a feathery look in other seasons.

APPLE. *Malus pumila.* Zones 3–8. Deciduous. 50 feet. Everybody thinks first of the apple as a fruit tree, but it is also a good ornamental, especially when it grows old and gnarled. If you want to grow apples for fruit, you must plant at least two different varieties that bloom at the same time. For ornament only, you need just one tree; but if your neighbors happen to have apples too, your tree will probably bear fruit unless you spray it with a chemical that prevents setting of fruit.

BEECH, AMERICAN. *Fagus grandifolia.* Zones 3b–9. Deciduous. 90 feet. Given the space it requires, the American beech develops into a magnificent, wide, rounded tree with massive trunk and branches and fine gray bark. The leaves turn light brown in the fall and hang on for a long time.

BEECH, EUROPEAN. *Fagus sylvatica.* Zones 5–10. Deciduous. 90 feet. The European beech is very similar to its American cousin but is available in many more varieties. Some have weeping branches. Some have dark purple or copper-colored leaves. Some have leaves that resemble small fern fronds.

Although only about 30 years old, this copper-leaved European beech is just a little taller than a two-story house but covers a wide area. Given another 100 years it will be three or perhaps even four times as large.

BIRCH, EUROPEAN. *Betula pendula.* Zones 2–10. Deciduous. 60 feet. Tl
European birches are lovely, graceful trees with white bark and nice
chiseled leaves that flutter in the breeze. There are several varietie
some with such pendulous branches that they might be mistaken at
distance for willows. But the true European birch is especially valuab
because it is slender and upright and has a delicately shaped structur
It grows fast.

BIRCH, WHITE. Also called Paper Birch and Canoe Birch. *Betula papyi
fera.* Zones 2–7. Deciduous. 90 feet. This is a sturdier-looking tree tha
the European birch. "Handsome" is a proper adjective for it. Its gliste
ing white bark stands out even against new-fallen snow, and when yc
plant it so the trunk is silhouetted against an evergreen background, I'ı
certain you'll agree that you've rarely seen anything more beautiful.

The white birch generally has a single trunk. Don't confuse it wit
the inferior gray birch, which usually has a cluster of trunks. Anoth
way to distinguish the gray birch is by its bark, which, though white,
a sort of dirty white with many more black spots than you find on
true white birch.

CEDAR, DEODAR. *Cedrus deodara.* Zones 7–10. Needled evergreen. 1(
feet. The deodar cedar forms a splendid pyramid with slightly pe
dulous branches covered with stiff needles in upright bunches. Tl
cones resemble tall, slender beehives of the old-fashioned type.

CEDAR-OF-LEBANON. *Cedrus libani.* Zones 7–10, but variety *stenocan*
grows in Zone 6. Needled evergreen. 120 feet. This historic tree forms
very picturesque pyramid with stiffly horizontal branches that droc
slightly at the ends. The leader is floppy, like a seated man who is ove
come with drowsiness.

*A slender European birch sheathed with ice. But even without this load tł
branchlets droop and sway in the slightest breeze. Behind it is a Norway spruc
one of the faster-growing conifers.*

A *Japanese flowering cherry in the spring is a mass of delicately colored flowers*

CHERRY, FLOWERING. *Prunus* species. Zones 4–10. Deciduous. 75 feet, but most varieties are smaller. The flowering cherries are afflicted with several problems, but they are so lovely—especially in bloom—that they merit a place in every garden. The white or pink flowers appear in the spring. The bark of some varieties is a glistening deep reddish color. Outstanding species are the Higan, Japanese and Sargent cherries.

CHINESE FLAME TREE. *Koelreuteria formosana.* Zones 9b–10. Deciduous. 30 feet. This is a good terrace tree because its innumerable small leaflets let the sun filter through. In summer it makes a brief show of yellow flowers, but it is most beautiful in the fall, when the entire crown is covered with large, papery, salmon-colored seed pods.

CORAL TREE, NAKED. *Erythrina coralloides.* Zone 10. Deciduous. 20 feet. This wide tree is of decorative value in winter because of its unusual structure with bending branches. Then from March to May it turns into a coral-red mass with interesting cone-shaped blossom clusters from which the mature flowers project like Christmas candles. In summer the large leaves appear. These turn yellow in the fall.

CORKTREE, AMUR. *Phellodendron amurense.* Zones 3b–10. Deciduous. 40 feet. This is a wide, rounded tree with enormous trunk and limbs that are covered with deeply fissured, corklike bark. Its light foliage makes it a fine tree for planting to shade a terrace.

CRAB APPLE. *Malus* species. Zones 2–10. Deciduous. 50 feet, but most species are smaller. Crab apples are shapely trees famed for their dense blanket of white, pink or red spring flowers. Many varieties have decorative red or yellow fruits, but the best in this respect are those with bright red, 2-inch fruits that are used to make delicious jelly.

CRAPE-MYRTLE. *Lagerstroemia indica.* Zones 7b–10. Deciduous. 25 feet. A lovely little tree in all seasons. Clusters of pink to red flowers in midsummer; yellow fall foliage. Excellent light-brown bark, which flakes off interesting angular trunks, is revealed in the winter.

CRYPTOMERIA. *Cryptomeria japonica.* Zones 6–10. Needled evergreen. 150 feet. The cryptomeria is pyramidal but has a billowy effect, and as it gets older, spaces develop between the branches to give it added beauty and informality. Its greatest fault in my part of the country is its tendency to turn a sickly brown in winter, and for that reason it isn't worth planting here. But in other areas it is green all the time. If a local

The cryptomeria forms a billowy pyramid that becomes more open and picturesque with age.

nurseryman tells you that that's the case where you live, by all means buy one of the trees.

DOGWOOD, FLOWERING. *Cornus florida.* Zones 5–9. Deciduous. 40 feet. An outstanding small tree, the flowering dogwood is known to almost everyone for its spring display of white or pink flowers. But the real gardener knows that it is excellent in all seasons. In the fall it is covered with bright red berries cherished by birds and squirrels. In summer and winter it is simply a well-shaped plant that shows off in every situation. It tolerates some shade but prefers sun.

DOGWOOD, JAPANESE. Also called Korean Dogwood. *Cornus kousa.* Zones 6–10. Deciduous. 20 feet. Although the Japanese dogwood is unfamiliar to many people, it is widely available and should be planted wherever it grows. Don't use it as a substitute for the flowering dogwood

A pair of Japanese dogwoods so densely covered with star-shaped white flowers that the branches are only barely visible. Although less well known than the flowering dogwood, it is every bit its equal.

but in addition to it. The flowers are white to creamy white and are shaped like four-pointed stars. The fall fruits resemble large strawberries. The tree tolerates a little shade.

ELM, CHINESE. *Ulmus parvifolia.* Zones 6–10. Deciduous. 60 feet. No elm is the equal of the great American elm, which has been almost wiped out by disease, but this Chinese relative is worth planting anyway. It's especially desirable if you need an extremely fast-growing tree. The true species is well shaped and has small clusters of flowers in late summer or fall. Variety *sempervirens* is known as the evergreen elm because it holds its leaves till new ones appear in the spring. Wide-spreading, it has weeping branches like the weeping willow.

FIR, WHITE. *Abies concolor.* Zones 5–10. Needled evergreen. 120 feet. The white fir is a pyramid with blue-green needles that contrast nicely with the deep green of other needled evergreens.

FRINGETREE. *Chionanthus virginicus.* Zones 5–9. Deciduous. 30 feet. The fringetree is related to lilacs but is larger and more rounded. In late spring it bears enormous clusters of fragrant white flowers. In fall the leaves turn yellow and there are clusters of small blue-black fruits.

FRINGETREE, CHINESE. *Chionanthus retusa.* Zones 6–10. Deciduous. 20 feet. The Chinese fringetree is smaller and a bit more shapely than our native tree and has so many white flower clusters that it looks as if it had been hit by a blizzard.

GINKGO. *Ginkgo biloba.* Zones 5–10. Deciduous. 120 feet. This ancient tree—one of the oldest on earth—is a tough specimen that thrives under adverse conditions. It develops into a picturesque structure with branches that are studded with little woody spurs that make an interesting outline against the winter sky. The unusual leaves are shaped like ladies' fans. Be sure to buy male specimens only; the females have a foul-smelling fruit.

GOLDEN-CHAIN TREE. *Laburnum watereri.* Zones 5–10. Deciduous. 30 feet. The golden-chain tree is shaped like a narrow vase. In late spring it drips with long, hanging, wisterialike clusters of bright yellow flowers.

GOLDEN-RAIN TREE. *Koelreuteria paniculata.* Zones 6–10. Deciduous. 10 feet. This flat-topped tree makes a brilliant show in early summer when it is covered with yellow flowers in very big, upright clusters.

GRAPEFRUIT. *Citrus paradisi.* Zones 9b–10. Broadleaf evergreen. 30 feet. The grapefruit tree grows as wide as high and has a dense coverage of lustrous leaves. The flowers are waxy white. The big yellow fruits borne in winter need no introduction. All in all, this is a beautiful and useful tree.

GUM, LEMON-SCENTED. *Eucalyptus citriodora.* Zones 9b–10. Broadleaf evergreen. 75 feet. This is one of the outstanding eucalyptus trees in the beauty department. It is tall, slender and open, clothed with yellow-green leaves that smell of lemons. The bark is whitish to pinkish.

GUM, RED-FLOWERING. Also called Flame Eucalyptus. *Eucalyptus filifolia.* Zones 9b–10. Broadleaf evergreen. 40 feet. The red-flowering gum is a neat, round-headed tree with a single short trunk. In summer it is a mass of red, orange, salmon or pink 2-inch flowers, which are borne in clusters such as you might buy from a florist as a bouquet.

GUM, SILVER-DOLLAR. *Eucalyptus polyanthemos.* Zones 8b–10. Broadleaf evergreen. 60 feet. Another excellent eucalyptus, often with several trunks covered with mottled bark.

HOLLY, AMERICAN. *Ilex opaca.* Zones 6–9. Broadleaf evergreen. 50 feet. You need no introduction to the glossy, spiny leaves and bright red berries. What you may not know is that the tree itself forms a well-shaped pyramid with foliage and berries growing from top to bottom. To have berries, you must plant both male and female trees.

Tall and vase-shaped, the golden-chain tree makes a brilliant show in mid-spring.

HOLLY, ENGLISH. *Ilex aquifolium.* Zones 6b–10. Broadleaf evergreen. 70 feet. If you live in the Pacific Northwest or other temperate region near a large body of water, plant a male and female English holly. This is rated the best of the genus, having very glossy leaves and very bright red berries in large clusters.

HONEYLOCUST, THORNLESS. *Gleditsia triacanthos inermis.* Zones 5–8. Deciduous. 130 feet. The Moraine honeylocust is the best variety. It grows fast and forms a very wide, flat crown clothed with tiny leaflets that move with every breath of air. An excellent tree for shading a terrace.

IRONBARK, RED. *Eucalyptus sideroxylon.* Zones 9–10. Broadleaf evergreen. 80 feet. This extremely variable tree grows in many shapes, so select it carefully before planting. The blue-green leaves turn bronze in the fall. Fluffy pink-to-red flowers hang in clusters from fall to spring. The bark is almost black.

JACARANDA. *Jacaranda acutifolia.* Zones 9b–10. Deciduous. 50 feet. This delightful tree has feathery foliage that flutters in the slightest breeze and large clusters of violet-blue flowers in spring and summer.

JAPANESE PAGODA TREE. *Sophora japonica.* Zones 5–10. Deciduous. 60 feet. The pagoda tree spreads wide, has feathery leaflets and is covered in late summer with upright pyramids of white flowers. Like another Oriental tree, the ginkgo, it does well in city smog.

LARCH, JAPANESE. *Larix leptolepis.* Zones 5–9. Deciduous conifer. 90 feet. All the larches are noted for their small, soft needles, which start out very bright green in the spring, turn yellow in the fall and then drop. But the Japanese larch is especially attractive. It grows as a slender pyramid.

LINDEN, LITTLELEAF. *Tilia cordata.* Zones 3b–10. Deciduous. 90 feet. A large, rounded tree with branches almost sweeping the ground, the littleleaf linden has dense, heart-shaped leaves and small but very fragrant whitish flowers in early summer. A handsome specimen anywhere.

An excellent tree for shade and ornament—the thornless honeylocust. It grows fast to form a wide-spreading, flat-topped crown.

Linden, silver. *Tilia tomentosa.* Zones 5–10. Deciduous. 90 feet. The silver linden forms a broad pyramid with a round top. Its heart-shaped leaves are white underneath, so when the wind blows, the entire tree looks silvery.

Madrone, Pacific. *Arbutus menziesii.* Zones 7b–10. Broadleaf evergreen. 100 feet. The Pacific madrone is a dirty tree forever dropping twigs and leaves, but you will forgive it this fault. It has good leathery foliage, peeling bark in two colors, white spring flowers like the lily-of-the-valley, and clusters of red-orange berries in fall and winter.

Magnolia, saucer. *Magnolia soulangeana.* Zones 6–10. Deciduous. 25 feet. The saucer magnolia has one or more trunks but is especially attractive with just one. In winter it forms an interesting picture featured by light-gray bark and velvety flower buds. In early spring it is hidden under huge white or pink cup-shaped flowers. The rest of the year it is just pleasantly green.

Magnolia, southern. *Magnolia grandiflora.* Zones 7b–10. Broadleaf evergreen. 90 feet. There are not enough superlatives for the southern magnolia. It grows into an enormous pyramid. The white, very fragrant, large flowers appearing in late spring and early summer are as big as dinner plates. The interesting seedpods split open to display gaudy red seeds in the fall.

Magnolia, star. *Magnolia stellata.* Zones 6–8. Deciduous. 20 feet. The star magnolia is a small tree with a charmingly irregular branching structure and light-gray bark. Its fragrant, white, multipetaled flowers come into bloom in very early spring. The dark-green leaves turn yellow or bronze in the fall.

Mango. *Mangifera indica.* Zones 9b–10. Broadleaf evergreen. 90 feet. It seems hardly proper for one tree to offer so much: beautiful form; very long, lance-shaped leaves that open purplish or reddish and turn glossy green; hanging clusters of pink flowers in the winter; delicious, peachlike yellow, red or greenish fruits in late spring and summer.

The saucer magnolia is popular mainly because of the large pink flowers that blanket it from top to bottom. But it is beautiful in all seasons, whether clothed with big leaves or displaying its irregular, gray-barked trunk and branches in winter.

MAPLE, AMUR. *Acer ginnala.* Zones 2–10. Deciduous. 20 feet. An excellent small tree with thick green leaves that turn scarlet in the autumn. The yellowish spring flowers are fragrant and are followed by bright red, winged seeds that stand out against the foliage.

MAPLE, NORWAY. *Acer platanoides.* Zones 3b–10. Deciduous. 90 feet. The Norway maple is planted so much that I almost hesitate to list it, but I must, because it's a fine tree with a rugged, rounded structure. The foliage is so dense that almost nothing will grow underneath. The yellowish-green flowers in spring have a pervasive fragrance.

A great many small varieties have been developed, and unfortunately they somehow all look gross. Worst of all are those with foliage that stays purple or dark red throughout much of the growing season. If you want to plant a Norway maple, stick to the original species. If you want red foliage, plant a Japanese maple.

MAPLE, SUGAR. *Acer saccharum.* Zones 3b–10. Deciduous. 120 feet. The sugar maple is probably the most colorful of autumn trees. It turns fiery red or deep orange and can be seen for miles. In all seasons it is distinctive for its shape and good foliage.

MIMOSA. Also called Silktree. *Albizia julibrissin.* Zones 7b–10, but variety *rosea* will grow in Zone 6. Deciduous. 35 feet. The mimosa is shaped something like an enormous parasol with a flat top. The leaves resemble fern fronds, giving the entire tree a feathery lightness, and throughout most of the summer it is covered with delicate pink flowers.

MOUNTAIN ASH, EUROPEAN. Also called Rowan Tree. *Sorbus aucuparia,* Zones 3b–8. Deciduous. 60 feet. Another tree with charming feathery foliage, the mountain ash is prized mainly for its enormous clusters of bright red berries in the fall. The flat flower clusters preceding the berries are white.

NORFOLK ISLAND PINE. *Araucaria excelsa.* Zone 10. Needled evergreen. 100 feet. This distinctive pyramidal conifer has horizontal branches that grow in widely spaced tiers. The needles are dark green and sharp.

OAK, BUR. Also called Mossycup Oak. *Quercus macrocarpa*. Zones 4–10. Deciduous. 100 feet. A fine oak for the Middle West, this rugged specimen has large branches that angle rather sharply upward. The leaves turn reddish-brown in the fall. The acorns are almost enclosed in mossy cups.

OAK, LIVE. *Quercus virginiana*. Zones 8–10. Broadleaf evergreen. 60 feet. Given time, a live oak will send its huge limbs so far to the sides that it shades not just one but two suburban lots. There are few more awe-inspiring yet friendly trees.

OAK, PIN. *Quercus palustris*. Zones 5–10. Deciduous. 75 feet. The pin oaks are slender and upright, with bottom branches that droop, middle branches that grow straight out and upper branches that are almost vertical. The leaves are fairly small, sharply pointed and turn brownish-red in the autumn.

OAK, VALLEY. Also called California White Oak. *Quercus lobata*. Zones 7–10. Deciduous. 70 feet. This is to California what the following tree is to the East. They are very similar.

OAK, WHITE. *Quercus alba*. Zones 5–10. Deciduous. 90 feet. Of all the oaks this is the mightiest and best. It's a huge, outreaching giant with a massive trunk and limbs as big as the trunks of lesser trees. The lobed leaves turn purple-red in autumn, and squirrels scamper everywhere collecting the small, sweet acorns.

OAK, WILLOW. *Quercus phellos*. Zones 6–9. Deciduous. 50 feet. The willow oak is small, almost dainty—quite unlike other oaks in size and shape. And to add to its distinction, it has leaves shaped like the willow's.

OLIVE. *Olea europaea*. Zones 8b–10. Broadleaf evergreen. 25 feet. A favorite ornamental in California, the olive has gray-green, willowlike foliage and a gnarled trunk with smooth gray bark. It produces bitter black fruits that must be pickled before they can be eaten, but you can avoid these if you wish by pruning or applying a hormone spray.

ORANGE. *Citrus sinensis.* Zones 9b–10. Broadleaf evergreen. 25 feet. The No. 1 citrus tree also deserves a top mark on any rating sheet of ornamental trees. The foliage is lustrous and dense, the white flowers deliciously fragrant, and those fruits—!

PALM, COCONUT. *Cocos nucifera.* Zones 9b–10. Broadleaf evergreen. 100 feet. There are many varieties of the coconut palm and all are beautiful as well as bountiful. Some, however, grow tall and slender, while others are quite short. In Florida, at the moment, planting should be restricted to the latter, because they are resistant to the disease which is killing the tall palms. Elsewhere in tropical climates you can plant any variety you like.

PALM, DATE. *Phoenix dactylifera.* Zone 10. Broadleaf evergreen. 60 feet. The date palm has a huge crown of arching fronds and a straight trunk studded with the remains of old fronds. The enormous flower clusters in the spring give way in the fall to even bigger hanging clusters of toothsome fruits. You must plant male and female specimens for fruit production.

PALM, MEXICAN FAN. *Washingtonia robusta.* Zones 9b–10. Broadleaf evergreen. 90 feet. The slender, curving trunk bears a topknot of big, coarse fronds that resemble a lady's fan with the ends of the ribs exposed. The bunch of dead fronds hanging just below the crown doesn't contribute to the beauty of the tree, but it's been popular for years in southern California.

PALM, ROYAL. *Roystonea regia.* Zones 9b–10. Broadleaf evergreen. 80 feet. This regal Florida palm has a long, smooth trunk with an unusual taper. It is surmounted by a big crown of fronds that hang downward at the bottom and grow upward at the top.

PEACH. *Prunus persica.* Zones 5–9. Deciduous. 25 feet. To me the peach looks like a small version of the beautiful mango. The foliage and form are not quite so refined, but the deep-pink flowers are exquisite, and the fruits are out of this world.

PERSIMMON, JAPANESE. *Diospyros kaki.* Zones 7b–10. Deciduous. 40 feet. Here is another very ornamental fruit tree. It is well shaped, covered with leathery leaves that turn orange or red in the autumn. The big, smooth, orange fruits are astringent but delicious and make a good show on the tree even after the leaves drop.

PINE, AUSTRIAN. *Pinus nigra.* Zones 4–7. Needled evergreen. 90 feet. The Austrian pine has a stiff, standoffish appearance but is very handsome. The long, dark-green, sharp-pointed needles glisten in the sun.

PINE, EASTERN WHITE. *Pinus strobus.* Zones 3–6. Needled evergreen. 150 feet. This is the most beautiful and most important of the pines. It starts out as a well-shaped pyramid but becomes flat-topped with age and may also be very irregular. The fine, flexible needles are a soft green, the cones slender, loose and up to 8 inches long.

PINE, LONGLEAF. *Pinus palustris.* Zones 8–9. Needled evergreen. 120 feet. An important timber species, the longleaf pine also merits a place in the yard because of its incredibly long, flexible, bright-green needles. The cones are also long—almost a foot.

PINE, SCOTCH. *Pinus sylvestris.* Zones 2–8. Needled evergreen. 75 feet. The Scotch pine is symmetrical in youth but is likely to become very erratic-looking—in a fascinating, decorative way—in old age. The needles are short, stiff and bluish-green. The bark is distinctly red.

PINE, WESTERN WHITE. *Pinus monticola.* Zones 6–8. Needled evergreen. 90 feet. Almost identical to the eastern white pine but grows in the West.

PLANE-TREE, LONDON. *Platanus acerifolia.* Zones 6–10. Deciduous. 100 feet. The London plane-tree has a close resemblance to our native sycamore but is more refined. It has flaking bark, large, attractive leaves, and brown, dried fruits in clusters of two or three. But its best feature is the fact that it thrives under the worst city conditions.

POINCIANA, ROYAL. Also called Flamboyant. *Delonix regia.* Zone 10. Deciduous. 40 feet. "Flamboyant" is the proper word for this large, umbrella-shaped tree. In spring and summer it is so sheathed with scarlet and yellow flower clusters that you can see it for miles. It also has fine foliage.

RED CEDAR, EASTERN. *Juniperus virginiana.* Zones 2–8. Needled evergreen. 60 feet. The red cedar grows so widely throughout the East and South that it's thought of almost as a weed tree. But don't underrate it as an easy-to-grow, undemanding, attractive ornamental.

RUSSIAN OLIVE. *Elaeagnus angustifolia.* Zones 2–9. Deciduous. 20 feet. A very tough tree, the Russian olive is nevertheless delightful in the garden because of its slender, gray-green leaves that move in the slightest breeze. Yellow-and-silver spring flowers are fragrant and are followed by yellow-and-silver berries in the autumn.

SCHEFFLERA. Also called Queensland Umbrella Tree. *Brassaia actinophylla.* Zones 9b–10. Broadleaf evergreen. 25 feet. Use the schefflera among other trees and shrubs for contrast. Its compound leaves are about the size of an umbrella, with each of the big, shiny leaflets taking the place of the ribs. In summer the tree bears arching clusters of red flowers, after which come purple fruits.

SEA-GRAPE. *Coccoloba uvifera.* Zones 9b–10. Broadleaf evergreen. 20 feet. This tough denizen of the seashore gives a bold, modern effect wherever it's grown. Its several trunks are angular and covered with mottled bark. The big, round leaves are thick and leathery—like an ensemble of straw fans flapping in the wind. The purple, grapelike fruits are used to make a jelly.

SNOWBELL, JAPANESE. *Styrax japonica.* Zones 6–10. Deciduous. 30 feet. This is an elegant flat-topped tree with horizontal branches which in the spring are covered on top with leaves and lined underneath with little white, bell-like flowers.

A young sweet-gum. The sharply pointed leaves turn brilliant red in the autumn.

SORREL TREE. Also called Sourwood. *Oxydendrum arboreum*. Zones 6–9. Deciduous. 75 feet, but normally smaller. A decorative tree when given a little room to develop, the sorrel tree has lance-shaped leaves that turn brilliant red in autumn. In early summer it is festooned with clusters of white flowers resembling lilies-of-the-valley.

SPRUCE, NORWAY. *Picea abies*. Zones 2–7. Needled evergreen. 150 feet. The fast-growing Norway spruce develops into a monumental pyramid with upward-curving branches that are weighted down by countless long, slender branchlets. The color is dark green. A fine sight in all seasons.

SPRUCE, SERBIAN. *Picea omorika*. Zones 5–7. Needled evergreen. 90 feet. The Serbian spruce is little known but worth hunting for far and wide. It develops into an incredible spire that looks slender enough to grace a New England church. The upward-curving branches drip with pendulous branchlets. The color of the tree is spruce green until the wind blows and shows the light-colored undersides of the needles.

STEWARTIA, JAPANESE. *Stewartia pseudo-camellia*. Zones 6–10. Deciduous. 60 feet. The Japanese stewartia is considered slightly inferior to the Korean species but is the only one that's readily available. And despite its No. 2 rating, it is all you can hope for in a small tree. It has handsome, two-colored, flaking bark, elliptical leaves that are purplish in the fall, and white, fragrant, camellialike flowers in early summer.

SWEET-GUM. *Liquidambar styraciflua*. Zones 6–10. Deciduous. 120 feet. The sweet-gum develops a pyramidal crown above a long, clear, straight trunk. The precise, star-shaped leaves turn an exciting red in the fall. The prickly brown fruits are beloved by flower arrangers.

TEA TREE, AUSTRALIAN. *Leptospermum laevigatum*. Zones 9b–10. Broadleaf evergreen. 30 feet. This is the perfect small tree to give your garden an Oriental look. It is best planted in the open, where it can exhibit its twisted trunks and branches topped with an umbrella of small oval leaves and white flowers in early spring.

THORN, WASHINGTON. *Crataegus phaenopyrum*. Zones 5–10. Deciduous.

The tulip tree grows to magnificent proportions but captures the eye at every age because of its handsome foliage and lovely greenish tuliplike flowers.

30 feet. The prickly Washington thorn is clothed with small white flowers in late spring and an incredible crop of red berries from fall well into winter. The leaves are triangular and look as if they had been chiseled by a craftsman.

TULIP TREE. Also called Yellow Poplar. *Liriodendron tulipifera.* Zones 5–10. Deciduous. 175 feet. This is the largest deciduous tree native to the United States—but don't let that stop you from planting it, because it's a stately beauty. The peculiarly shaped leaves form sizable fans that become yellow in the fall. In late spring single, yellow-green flowers resembling tulips appear here and there all over the tree.

Few trees are as symmetrical as the dense, dark-green umbrella pine (which grows at a snail's pace). The small evergreen in the foreground is a dwarf white spruce.

UMBRELLA PINE. *Sciadopitys verticillata.* Zones 6–10. Needled evergreen. 50 feet. The umbrella pine is incredibly beautiful and slow-growing. From a distance it is a dense, dark-green, slender pyramid. Close up, you are enthralled by the long needles that radiate from the twigs like the ribs of an umbrella.

WILLOW, GOLDEN WEEPING. *Salix alba tristis.* Zones 3–10. Deciduous. 75 feet. Willows have so many faults that I never find them easy to recommend. In fact, my wife planted one more or less over my dead body. But the weeping species are beautiful—this one especially so. It's a great billowing mound of slender, pendulous branches that are yellow the year round when young.

This weeping willow was only 6 feet tall when planted. Three years later it had attained this size. Although a troublesome tree in many ways, it is always charming. (Photo by Richard Beatty)

Yellow-wood. *Cladrastis lutea*. Zones 3b–9. Deciduous. 50 feet. The yellow-wood is a sturdy, shapely tree, excellent for shading a terrace. It has light-gray bark and leaves that turn yellow or orange in the fall, and every few years it's festooned in the spring with hanging clusters of fragrant, white, wisterialike flowers.

Yew, Hicks. *Taxus media hicksii*. Zones 3–10. Needled evergreen. 20 feet. The Hicks yew develops into a neat, narrow column if you keep it pruned; but left to itself, it is big and wide.

Selected Shrubs for Sunny Areas

Andromeda, mountain. *Pieris floribunda*. Zones 5–9. Broadleaf evergreen. 6 feet. Mountain andromeda isn't quite the equal of the Japanese species (see "Selected Shrubs for Shady Areas," Chapter 12), but it is definitely a good plant that you should consider. The flowers grow in upright clusters and appear in mid-spring.

Beautybush. *Kolkwitzia amabilis*. Zones 5–10. Deciduous. 12 feet. When not in bloom, you might think the beautybush is too big for the garden. But in late spring, when it's blanketed with pink flowers with yellow throats, you'll wish it were even larger.

Blueberry, highbush. *Vaccinium corymbosum*. Zones 5–7. Deciduous. 12 feet. Plant blueberries for beauty, fruit or—better still—for both. A very ornamental plant, the highbush blueberry has dense branches and twigs that zig and zag in a most attractive fashion and develop a pretty reddish cast in winter. The foliage turns scarlet in the autumn. Flowers in mid-spring are little white or pinkish bells. And then come those tasty blue berries in summer; but to have these, you must plant two different varieties together.

Bridal wreath. *Spiraea vanhouttei*. Zones 5–9. Deciduous. 6 feet.

The beautybush grows large and needs more pruning than it is usually given just to keep it within bounds. But it makes a lovely mass of color in the spring and serves as a dense screen plant even in winter when it is bare.

The Warminster broom is a mass of swirling brilliant green twigs in winter and is then completely hidden under yellow flowers in spring.

Bridal wreath is a fast grower with arching branches and profuse white flowers in late spring.

Broom, Warminster. *Cytisus praecox.* Zones 6–10. Deciduous. 6 feet. In winter this fascinating shrub is an irregular mound of bright green, upright, swirling twigs. Then, come spring, it turns into a mass of yellow flowers that are so profuse you can't see the green beneath.

BUTTERFLY BUSH. *Buddleia davidii.* Zones 6–10. Deciduous. 8 feet. The butterfly bush is an upright shrub with arching branches and big spikes of fragrant purple, blue, red, pink or white flowers from midsummer till fall.

CASSIA, FEATHERY. Also called Wormwood Senna. *Cassia artemisoides.* Zones 9–10. Broadleaf evergreen. 5 feet. A billowing shrub with silvery needlelike leaves, feathery cassia becomes a fountain of yellow flowers in winter and spring and even into the summer.

CEANOTHUS, POINT REYES. *Ceanothus gloriosus.* Zones 7–10. Broadleaf evergreen. 2 feet. A California native, ceanothus is grown for its clusters of lavender-blue spring flowers. It spreads more than twice as wide as high and has feathery, dark-green foliage.

CHERRY, NANKING. *Prunus tomentosa.* Zones 2–10. Deciduous. 9 feet. This spreading shrub has innumerable branches that are lined almost from end to end with white or pink flowers in spring and then with edible red cherries in the summer.

CINQUEFOIL, SHRUBBY. *Potentilla fruticosa.* Zones 3–10. Deciduous. 4 feet. The cinquefoils are pleasant little shrubs useful for many purposes. They display a host of small yellow flowers from mid-spring till almost fall. There are several excellent varieties.

COTONEASTER, ROCKSPRAY. *Cotoneaster horizontalis.* Zones 5–10. Deciduous. 3 feet. This is a low plant with long, slender branches that grow far to the side, close to the ground. It is excellent for planting on a bank or overhanging a wall. It has tiny pale-pink flowers in late spring, showy red berries in the fall.

COTONEASTER, SPREADING. *Cotoneaster divaricata.* Zones 6–10. Deciduous. 6 feet. This is a more upright but wide cotoneaster with large leaves, pink spring flowers and red fall berries. Use it in shrubbery borders or as a hedge.

COTONEASTER, WILLOWLEAF. *Cotoneaster salicifolia.* Zones 6b–10. Ever-

Low-growing rockspray cotoneaster looks particularly attractive when planted at the top of a wall or bank and allowed to hang down over it, as here. The shrubs just above the corner of the wall are Pfitzer junipers. The flowering dogwoods are brilliant with snow-white blooms.

green in warm climates, deciduous elsewhere. 15 feet. Long, arching branches are clothed with willowlike leaves. White flower clusters appear in the spring, scarlet berries in the fall.

ELAEAGNUS, AUTUMN. *Elaeagnus umbellatus.* Zones 3b–8. Deciduous. 12 feet. Like other elaeagnus species, this is an informal, tough plant with lovely silvery foliage. It bears fragrant flowers in the spring and silvery berries—which later turn red—in the fall.

HIBISCUS, CHINESE. *Hibiscus rosa-sinensis.* Zones 9–10. Broadleaf evergreen. 15 feet. One of the great flowering shrubs, Chinese hibiscus produces enormous single, semidouble or double flowers in whites, pinks, red, yellows and oranges in the summer. The flowers last only a day, but new ones keep opening.

HONEYSUCKLE, WINTER. *Lonicera fragrantissima.* Zones 6–10. Deciduous in cold climates, evergreen in warm. 6 feet. This honeysuckle is a spreading plant with stiff leaves that are blue-green below, dull green above. It has very fragrant, white flowers in early spring, which are followed quickly by shiny red berries.

HYPERICUM, HIDCOTE. *Hypericum patulum Hidcote.* Zones 6b–10. Deciduous in cold climates, evergreen elsewhere. 3 feet. A wide, rounded shrub, hypericum puts on an excellent display of fragrant, yellow, 3-inch flowers from late spring to mid-autumn.

JUNIPER, MEYER. *Juniperus squamata meyeri.* Zones 5–10. Needled evergreen. 12 feet. Left to itself, the Meyer juniper becomes a massive plant with upreaching branches clad in short bluish-green needles. But it can be—and usually is—kept much lower.

LILAC, COMMON. *Syringa vulgaris.* Zones 3b–8. Deciduous. 20 feet. Lilacs are indispensable shrubs—favorites of all Americans since pioneer times. Though called a common lilac, this is an uncommonly attractive plant. Given space, it fills out to form a rather wide, rounded shrub with many upright stems and branches that are terminated, in the spring, with delicious-smelling clusters of purple, lilac, blue, white, pink or red flowers. Many varieties are sold. Some are called French lilacs.

LILAC, LITTLELEAF. Also called Daphne Lilac. *Syringa microphylla superba.* Zones 6–8. Deciduous. 6 feet. This is an unusual lilac because it develops into a mound twice as wide as it is high. It has deep-pink flower clusters in mid-spring and sometimes again in the fall.

LILAC, PERSIAN. *Syringa persica.* Zones 6–8. Deciduous. 6 feet. One of the smallest lilacs, the Persian has fragrant, pale-lilac flower clusters. These frequently cover the entire branches.

LILAC, SWEGIFLEXA. *Syringa swegiflexa.* Zones 6–8. Deciduous. 9 feet. Another excellent lilac with pale-pink flowers.

MANZANITA, STANFORD. *Arctostaphylos stanfordiana.* Zones 7b–10. Broadleaf evergreen. 6 feet. A California shrub, Stanford manzanita has crooked, smooth-barked branches with glossy foliage and clusters of small pink flowers in late winter and early spring. Reddish-brown berries are produced in the fall.

MOCK ORANGE, LEMOINE. *Philadelphus lemoinei.* Zones 6–9. Deciduous. 8 feet. Most of the mock oranges in established gardens are poor varieties that deserve extinction. But the Lemoine hybrids are choice, with fragrant single or double white flowers in late spring.

NINEBARK, EASTERN. *Physocarpus opulifolius.* Zones 2–8. Deciduous. 9 feet. Ninebark resembles spirea and is of value only because it is extremely hardy. It has dense clusters of tiny white flowers in late spring. A dwarf variety makes a good hedge.

OLEANDER. *Nerium oleander.* Zones 8–10. Broadleaf evergreen. 20 feet. An ever-popular shrub in warm climates, oleander can be used for many purposes in sunny parts of the yard. It forms a large, rounded plant with white, pink, red or yellow flowers clustered at the ends of branches and twigs. The bloom period runs from mid-spring to mid-autumn. All parts of the plant are poisonous to eat.

Swegiflexa lilac is a new species and an unusually fine one. This specimen has been in the ground only about four years but is 5 feet high and covered with fragrant pink flowers.

The mugo pine is variable in its growth habit but always useful. These specimens, if left to their own devices, will probably grow more than 6 feet tall (but they can be kept much lower by annual spring pruning). Others are more like ground covers.

PINE, MUGO. *Pinus mugo mughus.* Zones 2–9. Needled evergreen. 8 feet. The mugo pine is superb in foundation plantings, shrubbery borders, rock gardens and as hedges and ground covers. The plants are variable, some growing to their full height, others creeping across the ground. All have splendid dark-green foliage.

PINK POWDER PUFF. *Calliandra haematocephala.* Also identified as *C. inequilatera.* Zone 10. Broadleaf evergreen. 10 feet. Handsome shrub with leaves that turn from a coppery color to metallic green. The flowers are like big rose-pink powder puffs and appear through the fall and winter. Use the shrub as a specimen or espalier.

POMEGRANATE, DOUBLE-FLOWERED. *Punica granatum legrelleae*. Zones 8b–10. Deciduous. 15 feet. There's no fruit on this pomegranate, but you won't be resentful, since it forms an attractive plant with narrow, glossy leaves and large, double, orange-red summer flowers in profusion.

ROSE, SHRUB. *Rosa* species. Zones 4–10. Deciduous. 8 feet. The shrub roses differ from the ordinary garden varieties of rose (which are also shrubs but not used as such) in that they are generally hardier, larger and more informal in their habit. They have lovely single, semidouble or double flowers in red, pink, white, yellow or purple. Some are very fragrant. Some plants also have sizable red fruits, called hips, which you can make into jelly and syrup.

Old varieties of shrub rose generally bloom only in the spring. Newer varieties bloom more or less throughout the growing season. Use them anywhere. They also make good hedges.

ROSE OF SHARON. Also called Althea. *Hibiscus syriacus*. Zones 6–10. Deciduous. 15 feet. This is another shrub that has been improved by breeding. Rather upright in habit, it has large, mallowlike flowers in white, pink, red, blue or purple in late summer.

SMOKEBUSH. *Cotinus coggygria*. Zones 6–10. Deciduous. 15 feet. The smokebush is a conversation piece because it's covered for much of the summer with masses of feathery pink, purplish or yellowish plumes. These are so dense that they suggest billows of smoke.

TEA TREE, NEW ZEALAND. *Leptospermum scoparium*. Zone 10. Broad-leaf evergreen. 8 feet. The species is little grown, but there are several varieties—some as low as 2 feet—that are choice shrubs. The leaves are tiny, the flowers not a great deal larger. But in winter and spring there is such a profusion of bloom that the rest of the plant is hidden. Colors range from a warm red through pink to white.

WINTERBERRY. Also called Black Alder. *Ilex verticillata*. Zones 3b–8. Deciduous. 12 feet. The winterberry is not distinctive in warm weather; you might mistake it for any number of plants. But in a good year it is covered all winter with red holly berries. These are so thick that the

The winterberry, a holly, is at its peak when the snow is on the ground and its branches are laden with bright red berries.

whole plant is red. But to have them, you must put in both male and female specimens.

YELLOW ELDER. *Tecoma stans.* Zone 10. Broadleaf evergreen. 6 feet. One of the finest native shrubs, yellow elder is a lush mass of green, which in the autumn puts out showy clusters of bright yellow, trumpet-shaped flowers.

Selected Vines for Sunny Areas

	Deciduous or evergreen	Height (feet)	Climate zones	Comments
Bougainvillea	E	20	10	Very vigorous twining vine with blankets of flowers in vibrant colors.
Cat's-claw vine *Doxantha unguis-cati*	D or E	40	8–10	Climbs by tendrils that cling to anything. Brilliant big, yellow, trumpet flowers. Very fast growth.
Clematis	D or E	20	4–10	Grows by tendrils. Countless gorgeous species and varieties in many colors. Some are fragrant. Needs sun, but roots must be in shade.
Coralvine *Antigonon leptopus*	D or E	40	9–10	Climbs by tendrils. Masses of tiny pink flowers in fall.
Easter lily vine *Beaumontia grandiflora*	E	30	10	Semitwining. Fragrant white, lilylike flowers. Bold foliage. Needs sturdy support.
Grape *Vitis* species	D	60	3–10	Grows by tendrils. Rampant vine with good foliage and delicious fruits.
Rose, climbing *Rosa* varieties	D	15	5–10	Train by hand. Gorgeous flowers in white, pink, red or yellow.
Royal trumpet vine *Distictis riversii*	E	20	10	Climbs by tendrils. Light-purple trumpet flowers, glossy leaves. Very showy.
Silverlace vine *Polygonum aubertii*	D	20	5–10	Twining vine covered with small white flowers.
Wisteria, Chinese *Wisteria sinensis*	D	25	6–10	Twining vine with large, pendulous clusters of fragrant blue or white flowers.
Wisteria, Japanese *Wisteria floribunda*	D	25	5–10	Twining vine. Enormous flower clusters in blue, white, purple or pink.

11 Making and Remaking Lawns

Most garden remodelings involve a certain amount of lawn work. The old lawn may need to be remade because it has become thin, choked with weeds or so bumpy that it feels like a cobblestone street when you walk on it. A brand-new lawn may need to be built in space that was formerly devoted to flower beds or shrubs or that was simply an unkempt stand of weeds.

Whatever your reason for working on the lawn, do the heavy labor called for on your property first; then you won't have to worry about damaging the lawn as you move trees and shrubs in and out and around the garden. In cold climates (from Zone 7 northward) the best time for making or extensively remaking a lawn with grass seed is in late summer. Elsewhere the work should be done in the spring regardless of whether you use seeds, plugs or sprigs.

Preliminary steps in making and remaking a lawn

If the existing lawn or area that you want to turn into a lawn does not slope properly, or has hollows that are too deep to fill, or high spots that are too large to level, the first step in making a new lawn is to strip off the topsoil down to a depth of 4–6 inches and pile it to one side. Then bring the subsoil to the proper grade, mix superphosphate with it at the rate of about 1 pound per 20 square feet, add life if your soil test shows it's needed, and recover the area with an even layer of the topsoil. This is a large undertaking, obviously. In small areas I've done it by hand. But if you have an entire lawn to deal with, you'd be wise to employ a man with a bulldozer or front-end loader.

If regrading is not required, simply turn over the topsoil to a depth of 6 inches, or whatever the actual depth of the topsoil, with a rotary tiller. Go back and forth over the ground several times to chop the sod or other vegetation into small pieces.

No matter whether you do or don't regrade the area, make sure that the topsoil is of adequate depth and quality. On many properties it is not. For grass to develop a strong stand, the topsoil should be at least 4 inches deep—preferably more. If you lack this depth, buy additional topsoil. If the topsoil isn't reasonably rich or is very porous, add an inch or two of humus. If it's clay, add about an inch of humus and an inch of coarse sand.

Once you're satisfied with the condition of the topsoil, add lime or powdered sulfur as called for by your soil test (the soil for grass should have a pH of almost exactly 7.0). Then add a balanced inorganic fertilizer that is rich in nitrogen. For example, apply 20 pounds of 10-6-4 fertilizer per 1000 square feet; 11 pounds of 18-6-9; or 8 pounds of 24-9-5. Work the additives into the topsoil with your tiller. Then rake the area smooth and level. As you do so, remove whatever large stones and weeds you turn up. Bury chunks of sod below the topsoil.

Now let the soil settle for at least a week—two if possible. Don't walk on it during the time and try to keep dogs off too. If you don't follow this practice but sow seed or put down sod immediately after preparing the soil, the lawn will be very uneven and pitted.

Seeding a lawn

In cold climates lawns are generally started from seed. The following species of grass are most commonly used.

Bahia grass. Bahia grass is started only from seed. The quality isn't very good, but in southern coastal states the grass is well thought of because it requires little maintenance and thrives under dry conditions. Pensacola and Paraguay are the best varieties.

Bent grass. If you're willing to spend a great deal of time maintaining a sunny lawn, put in bent grass. When well established it looks like velvet plush. In the North it's the top grass for golf greens. The grass may be started from seeds or from plugs and sprigs (see page 160).

Buffalo grass. This is used only in dry sections of the Great Plains. It is extremely drought-resistant, fine-textured and dense, but it's grayish in summer and turns straw-colored in the fall.

Kentucky bluegrass. If there is a basic grass for cold climates, this is it. It's beautiful, vigorous and drought-resistant once established but is occasionally plagued with diseases. Merion Kentucky bluegrass is superior to ordinary bluegrass, and there are several others even better though less well known. These include Warren's A-20, Pennstar and Fylking. All require sun. The only bluegrass that does fairly well in shade is Warren's A-34, also a superior variety.

A lawn of bluegrass thrives in the northern California sun. The mounded shrubbery area was created to break the huge flat expanse.

This bluegrass lawn does well in the shade of trees only because the climate is cool and damp, the trees are kept thinned out, and the grass is regularly fertilized and watered.

Red fescue. This is the best shade grass for cold climates but also does well in sun. It's durable and fine-textured. Choice varieties include Chewings, Pennlawn and Jamestown. Don't confuse any of the red fescues with tall fescue, a coarse grass that is suitable only for playfields.

Redtop. Redtop is often found in grass-seed mixtures, but like ordinary rye grass, its only value is to fill in a lawn until better grasses take hold. It doesn't survive more than two years.

Rye grass. Depending on the variety, rye grass is either an annual or a perennial. It is often incorporated into grass-seed mixtures because it's cheap, comes up very rapidly and produces a green lawn while other grasses in the mixture are developing. Even so, it's a coarse, temporary grass that should generally be avoided. The exception is a new perennial variety called Manhattan. Don't hesitate to use mixtures containing it. You can even use it by itself if you live near the seacoast and have sandy soil.

Some gardeners prefer to sow their lawns to a single type of grass—for example, all bluegrass or all red fescue—because this produces an absolutely uniform stand. Most gardeners, however, use mixtures, because if one species develops trouble, the others that are unaffected will fill in for it. Be warned, however, that the grass-seed mixtures on the market are extremely variable in composition and quality. If you use one, be sure that it is especially recommended for your area by a nurseryman, garden-supply store or gardener you can trust (*not* the local supermarket, discount house or highway garden center). The mixture should also contain a high percentage of the best varieties.

When sowing grass seed, make sure that the soil is not too wet, because it won't rake out evenly. Scarify the ground lightly with a rake. Then divide the area into 1000-square-foot sections and weigh out the seed into small lots. Each lot should contain the amount recommended on the label for 1000 square feet.

If you sow seed by hand, mix each lot with a little dry sand or vermiculite to make it easier to spread evenly. Then sow the seed in one 1000-square-foot section at a time. Sow half of the seed in each lot in one direction—for example, as you walk from north to south; then sow the other half perpendicular to this—walking in an east-west direction.

You can also sow seed with a spreader, but the spreader must be clean and set for the type of seed you're using. This information should be printed on the package; if it isn't, don't guess—sow the seed by hand. You should also hand-sow seed if the package label doesn't give directions for your particular brand of spreader. Two final points to remember is using a spreader are that (1) you should not overlap the seeded strips and (2) you should close the spreader when you reach the end of the row and turn it around. Otherwise the grass will be thicker in the overlaps than elsewhere.

When the entire lawn area has been seeded, rake it lightly with the teeth and back of the rake. Try to cover the seed as much as possible with a fraction of an inch of soil—never more than one-quarter inch—but don't worry if a lot is left exposed.

Roll the lawn very lightly, just enough to press the exposed seed into the soil and smooth out the rake marks. Then sprinkle the lawn with a fine spray that doesn't dislodge the seed or soil, but apply enough water so it penetrates half an inch or more.

After seeding a slope, cover it with a light sprinkle of chopped straw to help prevent erosion. The alternative is to cover the slope with netting made for the purpose. Both the straw and netting will disintegrate and disappear after the grass is up.

It's not necessary to cover a flat lawn, but many people consider it a good practice because it helps to keep the soil from drying out and conceals the seeds from hungry birds. If you follow the practice, use chopped straw.

Water the lawn regularly until the grass is well up. Use a fine spray so you don't disturb the seeds or seedlings, and don't let the soil dry out very long between applications. When the lawn is established, the frequency of watering can be reduced, but you should see to it that waterings and rainfall add up to about 1 inch of water per week.

Don't mow the lawn until it reaches a height of almost 3 inches.

Starting a lawn from plugs or sprigs

This is known as vegetative planting, because instead of sowing seeds, you plant small rooted pieces of growing plants. The majority— but not all—of the grasses grown in warm climates are handled in this way.

The most popular species for warm climates are the following:

Bermuda grass. Some Bermuda grasses are coarse, others are fine-textured, dense and beautiful. These are very much like bent grass and in the South are used instead of bent grass on golf greens. Among the outstanding varieties are Tifdwarf, Santa Ana and No-Mow. The last is unusual because it is more tolerant of shade than other Bermudas.

Centipede grass. This grass requires less maintenance than any other warm-climate grass but is not very resistant to wear. It grows in

Bermuda grass is the choice for southern lawns.

light shade as well as sun. Usually planted vegetatively, it can also be seeded.

Manila grass. This is closely related to zoysia and looks and performs in much the same way. It grows particularly well in the shade in the mid-South.

St. Augustine grass. St. Augustine grows in sun or shade. It adapts to a wide variety of conditions but is very susceptible to damage by chinch bugs. Bitter Blue is a superior variety but should be used only on lawns that get little wear.

Zoysia. Zoysia is dense, springy and durable. A fine green in warm weather, it turns the color of a camel's-hair coat at the first sign of frost and doesn't recover until the weather really warms up. Though advertised for use in northern gardens, it should be used only south of a line from Philadelphia to San Francisco. Emerald is the best variety, Meyer just a notch below.

Soil preparation for a lawn that is to be sprigged or plugged is exactly like that for a seeded lawn. If you use sprigs—the more economical method, because sprigs are nothing more than tiny pieces ripped from sod—they must be planted one by one with a small trowel. Because zoysia is slow to spread, space its sprigs 4–6 inches apart in both directions. All other grasses are spaced 8 inches apart.

Plugs are 1-inch-wide pieces of sod which must also be planted with a trowel. For fastest results, space them 8 inches apart in both directions. Normal spacing, however, is 12 inches.

After sprigs and plugs are planted, sprinkle the lawn frequently and fertilize lightly every two to four weeks with a high-nitrogen balanced fertilizer to encourage the grass to spread rapidly.

Sodding a lawn

This is by far the most expensive way to build a lawn, but if you want a strong stand of grass immediately, it's the procedure to follow. It also has several other important advantages. You can establish a lawn at any time during the growing season—from early spring to mid-autumn. You can walk on the lawn—even roughhouse on it—within two or three weeks, as soon as the roots knit with the soil. You have no erosion problems. And if you start with quality sod—preferably one that is certified by the grower under a statewide certification program—you won't have any weeds to trouble you.

Maximum success depends on preparing the soil in the way previously described; you cannot simply lay the sod on bare ground. Planting should be done just as soon as the sod is delivered. However, you can hold it for twenty-four hours in cool weather if you pile it in small stacks, with ample air circulation around them, and cover them with damp burlap. Lay the sod to a string stretched across the lawn. Butt the ends and sides of the rectangles tightly together. The cross joints in adjacent rows should be staggered as bricks are staggered in a wall. Cut small pieces as you need them with a sharp spade or knife.

After all the sods are down, roll them lightly and then water well—for about three hours. Water regularly thereafter until the grass is rooted.

Most of the sod sold in the North is bluegrass. In the South, zoysia, Bermuda grass and St. Augustine grass are the species mainly sold.

Renovating an old lawn

If your lawn is thin or has isolated bare spots, there's no need to remake it completely unless the grade is poor. The best time to do the work is after you have killed the weeds by springtime applications of broadleaf weed killers and crabgrass killer such as Tupersan, which has no injurious effects on new grass. In warm climates, plant at once after the weeds are dead. In cold climates it's best to wait until late summer.

If you sow seed, cut the lawn close and run over it with a gasoline-powered lawn renovator that takes up embedded grass clippings, called thatch, and slices open the upper layer of soil. Then scatter the seed over the lawn at slightly less than the rate for a new lawn, and water it in heavily.

Sprigs and plugs are planted with a trowel wherever they are needed.

On sizable bare patches, loosen the soil to a depth of 4–6 inches with a spading fork, pulverize it with a rake, tamp it, and then plant seeds, sprigs or plugs.

If an old lawn feels bumpy underfoot, remove the thatch and spread finely screened topsoil with a rake. The new soil should not be more than half an inch deep; otherwise it may kill the existing grass. Apply fertilizer as you would on an established lawn, and water it in thoroughly. No further treatment is necessary if the grass is reasonably thick. But if the grass is thin, it's a good idea to scatter seed over it before fertilizing and watering.

In all renovation work it's important to seed, sprig or plug with the same grass that is in the lawn. If you don't, you will end up with a patchwork quilt. If you are unable to identify the old grass, use a mixture of seed.

In the gardener's lexicon a ground cover is any low-growing plant—other than grass—that covers the ground like a blanket. Such plants are used primarily in shady areas where grass doesn't grow, but they are also valuable in sunny places that are too steep—or sometimes too rough or too uneven—to be mowed. Many people substitute them for grass simply to reduce garden maintenance.

Directions for planting ground covers are given in the next chapter along with a list of the plants that grow in shade. Many also grow in the sun, as noted. The following, however, are strictly sun lovers.

Selected Ground Covers for Sunny Areas

	Deciduous or evergreen	Height (inches)	Climate zones	Comments
Crowberry *Empetrum nigrum*	E	6	3–6a	Black berries in fall.
Crown vetch *Coronilla varia*	D	18	5–10	Pink flowers in summer. Fast-growing.
Ice plant *Mesembryanthemum* and other genera	E	8	9–10	Glistening foliage. Unbelievably brilliant colors. Outstanding on steep slopes.
Juniper, Chinese *Juniperus chinensis sargentii*	E	18	5–10	Very tough: dogs can't wear it down. Fairly upright.
Juniper, creeping *Juniperus horizontalis*	E	15	5–10	Prostrate. Very tough. Several fine varieties.
Juniper, shore *Juniperus conferta*	E	12	6–10	Grows flat. Very tough.
Korean grass *Zoysia tenuifolia*	E	8	9–10	Velvety grass forming large ripples.
Lippia canescens	E	3	7–10	Blue-gray foliage. Lavender flowers.
Sandwort *Arenaria verna*	E	3	4–8	Resembles fine grass. Tiny white flowers.
Strawberry, Alexandria *Fragaria vesca*	Semi-E	6	6–10	Pretty little plants that do not spread; set close together. Delectable little fruits.
Thrift *Armeria maritima*	E	3	3–7	Dead ringer for grass. Pink flowers. Needs perfect drainage.

12 Improving Shady Areas

Shade is the bane of many gardeners, and on old properties it's often extremely troublesome because it blankets such a large area and/or is so heavy.

I well remember the house my parents owned when I was starting school. In front of the house there were two Norway maples that shaded the yard so well that only a narrow strip required mowing. In back there were a willow, a couple of enormous poplars, an old apple tree and a privet hedge that towered 15 feet high along the rear lot line. One part of the backyard was sunlit for some of the day; otherwise that yard was only a little brighter than the front. As a result, my parents, who loved gardening, did almost none. The place depressed them, and they moved out as soon as they could—into a new house without a single tree on the entire double lot.

I don't recommend my parents' inaction. For one thing, if shady areas are not attended to, they look even more unkempt than uncared-for sunny areas. For another thing, they are not all that difficult to make attractive. Many treatments are possible. Finally, it has been my experience that once you get shady spots under control, it takes less effort to keep them that way than sunny spots, because plants don't grow so profusely.

What is shade? Old-time gardeners use a confusing (and confused) assortment of terms to describe the intensity or extent of shade.

For example, when they say that a certain plant will grow in shade, they are usually thinking about an area that is never brightened by the sun (except possibly in winter) but is not terribly dark. Shade, to my way of thinking, is what you find under a Norway maple or in an old grove of pines.

Deep shade and heavy shade might be described as gloomy shade. It's the kind of shade you find close under the trunk of a horse chestnut tree or behind overgrown arborvitaes and hemlocks in a foundation border.

Light shade and partial shade are used interchangeably, but it would be simpler for everyone if they weren't. I like to think of light shade simply as the absence of sunlight. It's the shade created when a thick white cloud passes across the sun. Partial shade, on the other hand, lasts only part of the day and then gives way to sunlight. An area that is exposed to the sun only in the morning or in the afternoon is partially shaded; occasionally it is said to be in half shade or broken shade.

Filtered and dappled shade are almost but not quite synonymous. Both are shade mixed with sunlight. But filtered shade is the very light shade you get when the sun shines through several layers of cheesecloth or through a honeylocust tree. By contrast, dappled shade is like a giraffe with the colors reversed—shade broken by splotches of sunlight.

All of this may seem academic, but it does make a difference to the gardener when he is coping with a shady area, because it helps to determine what he should plant. A great many plants grow in light, partial, filtered or dappled shade. Some require it, but others—those that are essentially sun lovers—just tolerate it. The same thing is true of the much more limited list of plants that grow in ordinary shade: some require it; others—those that require only some shade—just tolerate it. But very few things grow in deep shade.

Characteristics of shady areas. In addition to coping with the lack of sunlight, you should consider several other problems when you undertake to improve the shady areas on your property.

1. The areas are damp. Those in deep shade, of course, are damper than those in light shade; but all are damper than sunny areas. As a result, plants that are unusually susceptible to attack by mildew and other fungus diseases should be avoided.

2. The soil tends to be acid. Here again, deep shade is more trouble-some than light shade. But in either case it makes a difference in what you plant.

Have the soil tested first. If it is indeed acid, you should either stick to plants that require acid soil, or if you prefer to put in nonacid plants, you must mulch them with oak leaves or mix powdered sulfur into the soil. (See Chapter 3.)

3. The roots of the trees casting shade will compete vigorously with whatever small plants you put in. To assure the sturdy growth of the latter, you should therefore apply more fertilizer and water than you would otherwise.

4. Leaves falling from the trees are difficult to rake up if the ground underneath is carpeted with plants. In time, of course, the leaves wither, sink down and disappear in the carpet; but until then the area is a mess.

For instance, I have a large Norway maple that casts such heavy shade that except for a few wisps of moss, the ground underneath is bare and looks awful. But whenever I get girded up to planting the area with a ground cover, I remember my annual struggle to rake up the fallen maple leaves; and my enthusiasm wanes. If I were to put in pachysandra or periwinkle—both of which grow in the immediate vicinity—raking would be impossible. So I am now in the process of planting deciduous ferns, which grow luxuriantly in the summer but die down shortly before the maple starts to shed.

Planting grass. Too many people try to grow grass in shade because it seems the simplest thing to do. It isn't. Grass dislikes shade as much as the cacti that beautify the desert.

To be sure, there are certain species that are tolerant of shade. These include red fescue, centipede grass, Manila grass, St. Augustine grass, zoysia and one variety of Bermuda grass. But even they can be counted on only in partial, filtered or dappled shade.

Planting ground covers. If you want a solid mass of low-growing greenery in a shady area, a ground cover will do far better than any grass. Most of the types that tolerate shade (some ground covers need sun) do well in everything from the lightest filtered shade to ordinary shade. They draw the line only at deep shade.

In addition to being shade lovers, these ground covers are very attractive in themselves and are often used as a background for small spring bulbs that are planted to pop up among them. They also are durable and resistant to wear. Their only drawback is that large leaves from the trees overhead rest on the surface until they disintegrate. (On the other hand, small leaves, conifer needles, fruits and nuts soak right in.)

For best results, plant ground covers in the spring. Prepare the soil as for a lawn. Take pains to remove all weeds and grass clumps. For fast coverage of the ground, set the plants 4–6 inches apart. Keep them well watered until they take hold. Fertilize them about a month after planting and again about six weeks later. If you use a balanced inorganic food, water it in heavily so that it will not burn the leaves or roots. Or use dried manure; it does not have to be watered in. Pull out weeds as you see them: they are likely to be something of a nuisance until the ground cover fills out and conceals the soil, but are little trouble thereafter.

To keep a ground cover from spreading into a lawn or other area where you don't want it, surround it with metal curbing 4–6 inches deep, or use bricks set on end. The latter are particularly good because they serve as a mowing strip.

The following ground covers are among the best for shady areas. Many also grow in the sun.

Selected Ground Covers for Shady Areas

	Deciduous or evergreen	Height (inches)	Climate zones	Comments
Ajuga Bugle	E or D	8	5–10	Spikes of blue flowers in spring. Try planting bulbs amongst them. Partial or filtered shade or sun.
Bearberry *Arctostaphylos uva-ursi*	E	4	2–10	Glossy leaves turn red in winter. Pinkish-white flowers in spring; red berries in fall. Filtered shade or sun.

Pachysandra grows vigorously even in the dense shade of a horse chestnut tree. It is an outstanding ground cover—and easy to propagate.

	Deciduous or evergreen	Height (inches)	Climate zones	Comments
Bunchberry *Cornus canadensis*	D	6	3–6	A dogwood. White spring flowers; red berries in fall. Acid soil. Light shade.
Candytuft *Iberis sempervirens*	E	6	4–10	Blanketed with white flowers in spring. Very light shade or sun. Use in formal areas.
Ceanothus griseus horizontalis compacta	E	12	8–10	Grows in California. Blue flowers in spring. Partial shade or sun.
Cotoneaster, bearberry *Cotoneaster dammeri*	E	12	7–10	Red berries in fall. Partial shade or sun.
Cotoneaster, rockspray *Cotoneaster horizontalis*	D	24	6–10	Red fall berries. Best on slopes. Partial shade or sun.
Creeping lilyturf *Liriope spicata*	E	8	6–10	Lilylike leaves; blue flowers. Mow in early spring. Sun or light shade.
Dichondra repens	E	3	9–10	Popular grass substitute in California. Tiny rounded leaves. Can be mowed for a very even carpet. Light shade or sun.
Epimedium	E or D	9	6–10	Several good species. Profuse red, white or yellow spring flowers. Light shade.
Ginger, wild *Asarum caudatum*	E	8	5–10	Very lush heart-shaped leaves. Partial or filtered shade.
Ivy, English *Hedera helix*	E	12	6–10	One of the best. Handsome dark-green foliage. A vine, it spreads widely. Grows in sun and all but deepest shade.
Lily-of-the-valley *Convallaria majalis*	D	8	3–8	Deliciously fragrant white flowers in spring. Partial or filtered shade.
Lingonberry *Vaccinium vitis-idaea*	E	12	2–10	Red berries in fall. Acid soil. Filtered or partial shade. Also grows in sun in cold climates.
Mahonia repens	E	12	6–10	Yellow spring flowers; black berries in fall. Partial shade or sun.

	Deciduous or evergreen	Height (inches)	Climate zones	Comments
Mondo grass *Ophiopogon japonicus*	E	6	7–10	Long, narrow, arching leaves. Lilac flowers in summer. Leaves can be raked off easily. Light shade or sun.
Pachysandra terminalis	E	12	4–10	Outstanding. Leaves in neat whorls. Inconspicuous white spring flowers. Tolerates anything but heavy shade.
Partridgeberry *Mitchella repens*	E	4	3–6	Fragrant white spring flowers; red fall berries. Filtered shade.
Paxistima canbyi	E	12	6–10	Charming, glossy leaves. Filtered or partial shade or sun.
Periwinkle *Vinca minor*	E	8	4–10	Outstanding. Very dark, glossy leaves. Blue flowers in spring. Sun or shade.
Plumbago *Ceratostigma plumbaginoides*	D	8	7–10	Blue flowers in late summer. Partial or filtered shade.
Salal *Gaultheria shallon*	E	18	6–10	Pinkish-white flowers in spring. Acid soil. Filtered or partial shade.
Sarcococca hookeriana humilis	E	12	7–10	Rich, shiny leaves. Partial to fairly deep shade.
Saxifrage *Bergenia crassifolia*	E or D	18	4–10	Enormous rounded leaves. Pink or white flowers on long stems in spring. Light shade, but tolerates sun in cool areas.
Stephanandra incisa crispa nana	E	24	6–8	Fernlike foliage; white flowers. Partial shade.
Strawberry geranium *Saxifraga sarmentosa*	E	12	6b–10	Rounded leaves with white veins are red underneath. Light shade.
Wandering Jew *Zebrina pendula*	E	6	10	Purple and white foliage. Light shade.
Wintercreeper *Euonymus fortunei*	E	12	4–10	Leathery foliage. Orange berries in fall (sometimes). A clinging vine, it may take off up trees. Sun, filtered or partial shade.

	Deciduous or evergreen	Height (feet)	Climate zones	Comments
Wintergreen *Gaultheria procumbens*	E	3	2–10	White spring flowers followed by red fall berries. Filtered shade.

Periwinkle—another outstanding ground cover—does well in both shade and sun. It is used here to hide the foundation walls without blocking the low windows.

Planting ferns. No family of plants has more beautiful foliage than the ferns. The light-green fronds are as delicate and lacy as the loveliest feather, and they move with birdlike grace in the breeze. Use the plants in large masses or small clumps: they never fail to attract attention.

With some exceptions, ferns are more at home in shade than most other plants, and they require no attention. But they must be used where they will not be beaten down, because once the stems are snapped, they become a tangle. They start making growth early in the spring: the greenish-grayish fiddleheads formed by the fronds before they open are one of the first indicators that the winter is over. In the fall some species die down; others live on. But even the best of the evergreen species is not overly attractive in winter.

Unfortunately there are not many nurseries that sell ferns, but they are easily dug up from the wild if landowners give permission. The best planting time is in the fall or early spring. For fastest growth, prepare the soil as for a lawn. Set most plants about 1 foot apart; give big species more space. Except for moisture, they need little attention.

Many kinds are to be found in nature if you hunt for them. Use whichever appeal to you particularly. If you scatter them in among other plants in a shady area, there's no reason why you shouldn't use an assortment of species. But for the best effect, stick to one kind in a mass planting.

Selected Ferns for Shady Areas

	Deciduous or evergreen	Height (inches)	Climate zones	Comments
Christmas fern *Polystichum*	E	36	3–9	Many species growing in different parts of the country.
Cliff-brake *Pellaea atropurpurea*	E	12	3–8	Fronds turn from delicate green to purple-brown. Needs lime and lots of humus.

	Deciduous or evergreen	Height (inches)	Climate zones	Comments
Common polypody *Polypodium vulgare*	E	10	2–8	Grows among and over rocks. Prefers filtered or partial shade.
Hay-scented fern *Dennstaedtia punctilobula*	D	30	4–8	Fragrant, delicate fronds. Adapts to most conditions.
Japanese painted fern *Athyrium goeringianum*	D	24	5–10	Gracefully tapering fronds tinged with red.
Lady fern *Athyrium filix-femina*	D	36	3–10	Tall and vase-shaped. Puts out new fronds till late summer.
Maidenhair fern *Adiantum*	D	24	2–10	Different species in most parts of the country. Generally rated the most beautiful ferns. Need moist soil.
Osmunda	D	60	3–9	Among the best species are the royal, interrupted and cinnamon ferns. Hardy and handsome. Need much moisture and acid soil.
Ostrich fern *Matteuccia pensylvanica*	D	60	2–7	Handsome plants for a shrubbery border.
Shield fern *Dryopteris*	E	36	2–8	Numerous varieties coast to coast.
Thelypteris	D	40	2–9	Variable but very attractive family.
Woodsia	D	24	2–9	Several excellent species, all lovely and delicate. Form mats. Do best in dappled shade.
Woodwardia fimbriata	D	96	10	Grows in California. Lovely weeping habit.

Tall ostrich ferns form a dense background for a small lawn area. The base of the old multitrunked common lilac is surrounded with hostas, a shade-tolerant perennial often used as a ground cover.

Maidenhair ferns are among the supreme beauties of the useful fern family. The vines are clematis.

Planting shrubs. If you need something more than a low, spreading mass of plants in a shady area, you'll find it among the shrubs. Big plants, medium plants or little plants; deciduous plants, broadleaf evergreens or needled evergreens; flowering plants or foliage plants—they are all here.

Because of their size, shrubs cost more than other plants that grow in shade, but you need fewer of them. So buy the best; plant them in large holes in well-prepared soil (see Chapter 3); cover the soil around them with a 3-inch mulch of humus; and sit back and enjoy the fruits of your labor.

In the lists that follow I have tried to differentiate between plants that require shade and those that tolerate it. But remember this about all flowering shrubs (as well as about trees and vines): the shadier the area, the less profuse flowering will be.

Selected Shrubs for Shady Areas

ABELIA, GLOSSY. *Abelia grandiflora.* Zones 6–10. Evergreen in warm climates, deciduous elsewhere. 6 feet. Slender, arching branches with glossy leaves that turn bronze in autumn. Small clusters of white-to-pink flowers in summer. May die to the ground in very cold weather but will come back rapidly. Prefers sun but does well in filtered or partial shade.

ANDROMEDA, JAPANESE. *Pieris japonica.* Zones 6–9. Broadleaf evergreen. 9 feet. This comes close to being my favorite shrub simply because it is so adaptable and handsome the year round. The plant forms a large, rounded mass with branches from the ground up. The leaves are dark green and glossy, the new leaves in spring reddish-bronze. The entire plant is blanketed in very early spring with pendulous sprays of creamy-white, lily-of-the-valleylike flowers. In winter the plant has a definite reddish look, because the flower buds hang from red stems. Grows best in sun, but don't hesitate to use it in filtered or partial shade.

ARBORVITAE. *Thuja.* Zones 6–10, but can be grown as far north as Zone 2 if you don't object to its brown winter color. Evergreen. The American arborvitae is a tall tree that has produced many dwarf varieties used as shrubs. Naturally of rather stiff habit (which can be made even stiffer by shearing), the shrubs are best used in foundation borders and wherever formality is appropriate. Grow in partial shade or sun. The best varieties include:

T. occidentalis globosa. 5 feet. Globe-shaped.

T. occidentalis umbraculifera. 4 feet. Starts out globe-shaped but develops a flat top.

T. occidentalis woodwardii. 8 feet. Rounded when young, but forms a huge, spreading mound with the passing years.

AUCUBA, JAPANESE. *Aucuba japonica.* Zones 7b–10. Broadleaf evergreen. 10 feet. A wide, vigorous plant with big, glossy leaves, dark-red flowers in spring and brilliant red berries in fall and winter. There are several good varieties with solid or variegated leaves. One of the favorites is the gold-dust plant, with leaves splotched with gold. Aucuba requires shade and even tolerates rather deep shade. Berries are produced on female plants only if you have a male plant nearby.

AZALEA. *Rhododendron* species. Azaleas are magnificent shrubs with blooms in almost all colors of the rainbow in the spring. Some are deliciously fragrant. All require partial shade. An ideal situation has sun for part of the day but not at midday. The plants should also be protected from the wind.

Despite their beauty, azaleas do not demand extraordinary attention. The soil, however, should be acid and kept mulched at all times with oak leaves or pine needles. Fertilize with cottonseed meal or other plant food formulated specifically for azaleas and rhododendrons. Snap off spent flowers immediately to encourage maximum bloom the following year. If a plant is not bushy enough, nip off the leaf buds.

Choice species and hybrids include the following:

Exbury hybrids. Zones 6b–10. Deciduous. 10 feet. Very large single flowers in clusters of as many as thirty. White, pink, red, yellow and orange.

Flame azalea. *R. calendulaceum.* Zones 6–10. Deciduous. 15 feet. Clusters of yellow, orange or red flowers.

Ghent hybrids. Zones 5–10. Deciduous. 10 feet. Single or sometimes double flowers in clusters. White, pink, red, orange, yellow. Very hardy.

Indian hybrids. Zones 8b–10. Broadleaf evergreen. 6 feet. Large clusters of white, pink, red or violet flowers in early spring. Needs very little sun. Filtered shade is good.

Azaleas like sun for part of the day but partial shade at midday.

Knap Hill hybrids. Zones 6b–10. Deciduous. 10 feet. Very similar to Exbury hybrids.

Kurume azalea. R. *obtusum.* Zones 7–10. Broadleaf evergreen. 3 feet. Almost completely blanketed with small white, pink or red flowers.

Mollis hybrids. Zones 6–10. Deciduous. 5 feet. White, yellow, orange, pink or red flowers up to 4 inches across, in clusters.

Royal azalea. R. *schlippenbachii.* Zones 5–10. Deciduous. 15 feet. Fragrant pink flowers in small clusters.

Snow azalea. R. *mucronatum.* Zones 6b–10. Broadleaf evergreen. 6 feet. Fragrant white flowers in small clusters.

Torch azalea. R. *obtusum kaempferi.* Zones 6–8. Evergreen in warm climates, almost deciduous elsewhere. 10 feet. Innumerable fiery red flowers. Can withstand rather deep shade.

BAMBOO, YELLOW-GROOVE. *Phyllostachys aureosulcata.* Zones 6b–10. Broadleaf evergreen. 25 feet. Though it grows in cold climates, this is a true bamboo with slender green canes grooved with yellow. Plant it where it will sway in the breeze, or against a wall, where the canes and slender leaves will show up in silhouette. Like a great many bamboos, this spreads rapidly in every direction and will soon take over your yard if you don't cut back the roots regularly. The alternative is to surround the roots with an 18-inch-deep underground wall of bricks or metal. Give filtered shade or sun.

BARBERRY, JAPANESE. *Berberis thunbergii.* Zones 5–9. Deciduous. 7 feet. One of the most commonly grown barberries, this plant prefers sun but does very well in shade. It turns bright red in the fall and is covered with red berries from fall through winter. An excellent dwarf variety is the box barberry (*B. thunbergii minor*).

BARBERRY, WINTERGREEN. *Berberis julianae.* Zones 6–9. Broadleaf evergreen. 6 feet. A very thorny shrub with long, slender, spiny-edged leaves. It has little bright-yellow flowers in the spring and black berries in the fall. Give partial or filtered shade or full sun.

BOX, COMMON. Also called Boxwood. *Buxus sempervirens.* Zones 6b–10. 20 feet. Box is dense and dark green and usually develops into a big, rounded plant, but it can be sheared. It is too formal for the ordinary shrubbery border containing mixed species but is excellent standing more or less alone and used as an accent. Little attention is required except in winter, when you should relieve it of whatever heavy snow covers it. Grow in light shade or sun.

There are many varieties. Edging box (*B. sempervirens suffruticosa*) is one of the best, reaching only 3 or 4 feet. Vardar Valley and Inglis are also good.

BOX, KOREAN. *Buxus microphylla koreana.* Zones 5b–10. Broadleaf evergreen. 4 feet. Not quite as fine as the common box, but the hardiest of all varieties.

A woodland garden planted with azaleas.

CAMELLIA, COMMON. *Camellia japonica.* Zones 7b–10. Broadleaf evergreen. 10 feet. Camellias are among the truly outstanding flowering shrubs. Their large lovely flowers, ranging from white through pink to red, appear from fall into late winter. The leaves are glossy green. The list of beautiful varieties goes on and on. The plants need a slightly acid soil and should be kept mulched and watered. In 50 or 100 years they will grow into sizable trees unless pruned occasionally.

CAMELLIA, SASANQUA. *Camellia sasanqua.* Zones 7b–10. Broadleaf evergreen. 10 feet. This camellia is a little less showy than the foregoing, but valuable because it blooms much earlier in the fall. It also will grow quite large if you don't restrain it.

CAROLINA ALLSPICE. Also called Sweetshrub. *Calycanthus floridus.* Zones 5–10. Deciduous. 9 feet. Handsome, aromatic leaves turn yellow in the fall. The unusual flowers are very fragrant, dark red, and appear in mid-spring. Partial shade or sun.

CHOKEBERRY, RED. *Aronia arbutifolia.* Zones 3–9. Deciduous. 9 feet. Pinkish-white flowers in dense clusters in mid-spring are followed by bright red berries that last from fall into the winter. The shrub is not attractive enough to be displayed prominently but is an addition in the background of any shrubbery planting. Partial shade or sun.

DEUTZIA, SLENDER. *Deutzia gracilis.* Zones 5–9. Deciduous. 3 feet. Slender deutzia is a pleasant little shrub with arching branches, but its main claim to fame is its blanket of white flowers in mid-spring. It needs partial shade or sun.

ELAEAGNUS, THORNY. *Elaeagnus pungens.* Zones 7b–10. Broadleaf evergreen. 12 feet. This is a tough, fast-growing shrub for partially shaded areas. It also grows in the sun. The leaves are silvery underneath, and when the wind blows, the entire plant turns to silver. Fragrant, silvery-white flowers hang from the thorny branches in the fall. In spring there are brown-to-red berries.

ENKIANTHUS, REDVEIN. *Enkianthus campanulatus.* Zones 5–10. Deciduous. 20 feet. Although not well known, redvein enkianthus is an excellent shrub forming a wide, upright column if you prune it occasionally. In spring it is covered with clusters of yellow-orange, lily-of-the-valley-like flowers with red veins. In the fall the entire plant turns scarlet and is one of the brightest spots in the landscape. Grow in filtered or partial shade or in sun.

EUONYMUS, EVERGREEN. *Euonymus japonicus.* Zones 8–9. Broadleaf evergreen. 15 feet. This is an attractive shrub with lustrous leaves, which in some popular varieties are variegated. It's useful in light shade as well as sun. In the fall there arc little pink and orange fruits.

EUONYMUS, WINGED. *Euonymus alatus.* Zones 3b–8. Deciduous. 10 feet. In full sun this is a superlative shrub; in filtered to light shade it is still excellent but does not turn such a beautiful rosy-red in the fall. The plant gets its name from the fact that its many branches, growing every which way, are lined from end to end with longitudinal corklike wings. I recommend it highly—but only if you can find someone who will let you dig up the numerous seedlings thrown off by a plant over ten years old. New strains offered in nurseries are coarse-looking—an unnaturally brilliant red—and they often lack wings on the bark.

FALSE CYPRESS. *Chamaecyparis.* The false cypresses are marvelous large trees, but through accident and the intervention of man, they have produced many dwarf varieties that are used as shrubs. All grow in partial shade and sun. Because they are densely clothed with tiny needles —which in some varieties are borne in fan-shaped sprays—they lend themselves to shearing; but they are more effective if allowed to grow naturally. The following are choice:
Dwarf Hinoki false cypress. *C. obtusa nana gracilis.* 4 feet. Zones 5–9. Dark, lustrous needle sprays.
Ellwood false cypress. *C. lawsoniana ellwoodii.* Zones 6–9. 6 feet. Silvery-blue foliage. Forms a compact column.
Fernspray false cypress. *C. obtusa filicoides.* Zones 5–9. 15 feet. Medium-green needle sprays. The graceful limbs have an Oriental look.
Forsteck false cypress. *C. lawsoniana forsteckensis.* Zones 6–9. 4 feet. Spreads to 6 feet. Dark green.

Slender Hinoki false cypress. *C. obtusa gracilis.* Zones 5–9. 20 feet. A very choice slow-growing plant with somewhat pendulous branches.

FATSHEDERA. *Fatshedera lizei.* Zones 7b–10. Broadleaf evergreen. 7 feet. A very handsome foliage plant with big leaves shaped like English ivy or the sweet gum tree. It tends to climb and therefore needs to be staked. Grows in anything from partial to deep shade.

FATSIA, JAPANESE. *Fatsia japonica.* Zones 7b–10. Broadleaf evergreen. 8 feet. This is one of the parents of fatshedera and is even handsomer. The dark-green, shiny, lovely leaves are as large as 15 inches across. The plant is completely happy in deep shade and also does well in lighter shade. For best effect, plant it by itself in front of a wall.

FIRETHORN, LALAND'S SCARLET. *Pyracantha coccinea lalandei.* Zones 6b–10. Evergreen in warm climates, deciduous elsewhere. 10 feet. Although it does better in full sun, firethorn is quite at home in partial or filtered shade. It is a top-notch shrub which you will like especially if you train or espalier it against a wall (but wear heavy gloves when you work on it because it's covered with thorns). In late spring it bears clusters of little whitish flowers. Then in the fall come large clusters of showy orange berries.

FORSYTHIA, BORDER. *Forsythia intermedia.* Zones 6–8. Deciduous. 9 feet. The best varieties of this forsythia—Beatrix, Lynwood Gold, Spectabilis and Spring Glory—have almost blindingly brilliant golden flowers in the spring; and from a distance the entire shrub looks like a sunburst. This is the main reason for planting it. But unfortunately the display is nowhere nearly as good in filtered-to-light shade as in full sun. So if you use it in a shady area, do so only because it grows like a weed and forms a solid screen of light green.

FOTHERGILLA, ALABAMA. *Fothergilla monticola.* Zones 6–9. Deciduous. 6 feet. Fothergilla requires partial shade. If possible, plant it in with evergreens so it can show off its yellow, orange and red fall dress to best advantage. In spring it has interesting thimblelike clusters of white flowers.

FUCHSIA. *Fuchsia* species. Zones 7b–10. Deciduous or evergreen. 12 feet. The flowers of the many variable varieties and types of fuchsia are so exquisite—white and lovely shades of red, blue and purple—that you're bound to want to grow them if you live in a warm climate. However, you must not count on the results you would get if you were living in California. That's fuchsia paradise. Plant in filtered or dappled shade and protect from wind. The soil should be a little acid.

HAWTHORN, INDIAN. *Raphiolepis indica.* Zones 7b–10. Broadleaf evergreen. 5 feet. Outstanding shrub with shiny, leathery leaves and masses of small blossoms followed by black fruits. The species is less desirable than the many varieties that have been developed. The flower color ranges from white to pink to rose. Prefers sun, but is worth growing in light shade.

HAWTHORN, YEDDO. *Raphiolepis umbellata.* Zones 7b–10. Broadleaf evergreen. 10 feet. This is a very ornamental shrub with black-green leaves, fragrant white flowers in upright clusters in late spring, and blue-black berries in fall and winter. It grows a little less densely in light shade than in sun.

HEAVENLY BAMBOO. *Nandina domestica.* Zones 8–10. Broadleaf evergreen. 8 feet. Although not a true bamboo, this shrub looks like it, and is even more effective when planted where the canes are silhouetted and can move in the wind. The foliage is delicate—pinkish when young, then light green, and finally red in the fall. White flowers in early summer form large clusters and then give way to loose clusters of bright red berries in the fall and winter. The shrub does best in sun but is perfectly happy in filtered or partial shade. In the Southwest it needs shade.

HEMLOCK, SARGENT WEEPING. *Tsuga canadensis pendula.* Zones 3–7. Needled evergreen. 10 feet. Sargent weeping hemlock is one of the world's most interesting and beautiful shrublike trees. Umbrella-shaped, it becomes in time a huge green igloo under which your children can play in complete privacy. It grows in filtered or partial shade or sun.

HOLLY, CHINESE. *Ilex cornuta.* Zones 7b–10. Broadleaf evergreen. 10

feet. Chinese holly is one of the very best hollies, and although it prefers sun, it still gives a good account in filtered or dappled shade. The leaves are large, dark green and usually have five spines. The berries in fall and winter are a brilliant red and unusually big. Burford holly is a superb variety.

HOLLY, JAPANESE. *Ilex crenata.* Zones 6–10. Broadleaf evergreen. 20 feet. Japanese holly is less spectacular than its relatives but in many ways more useful. The small oval leaves look like boxwood and are very dense. The plants range from low, wide varieties to tall, upright varieties. Convex Japanese holly (*I. crenata convexa*) is one of the low, rounded types and is especially valuable in the garden. Heller's holly is much smaller— a first-class plant for the front of a shrubbery border and in informal hedges. Grows in filtered or partial shade or sun.

HONEYSUCKLE, TATARIAN. *Lonicera tatarica.* Zones 3b–10. Deciduous. 9 feet. Tatarian honeysuckle is an easygoing, fast-growing shrub with white-to-red flowers in late spring followed by shiny red flowers in summer. It makes a better display when given full sun but doesn't mind dappled shade.

HYDRANGEA, GARDEN. *Hydrangea macrophylla.* Zones 6–10. Deciduous. 12 feet. Although it grows fairly far north, the garden hydrangea is a reliable bloomer only from Zone 7 southward. In that part of the world it needs partial shade. The color of the showy big balls of flowers depends on the acidity of the soil. If the pH is much below 7.0, the flowers are blue; from pH 7.0 upward, the flowers are pink. You can control the color by giving the plants aluminum sulfate to make the flowers turn from pink to blue, or superphosphate to reverse the color change.

HYDRANGEA, OAKLEAF. *Hydrangea quercifolia.* Zones 6–10. Deciduous. 6 feet. This hydrangea is not as gaudy as the foregoing but is more attractive and useful. The big leaves are shaped like oak leaves and turn bronzy-red in the fall. The flower clusters are very large, irregularly shaped and brilliant white. Needs partial shade in warm climates and is quite at home in it farther north.

Mountain laurel (foreground) is superb in all seasons. Even in bitter cold it is a fresh, dark green. In late spring it is covered with great clusters of prettily shaped, pale-pink flowers. The trees are, left to right, a Norway maple, red pine and sycamore.

JUNIPER, PFITZER. *Juniperus chinensis pfitzeriana.* Zones 5–10. Needled evergreen. 10 feet. A mainstay of many gardeners, Pfitzer juniper thrives with little attention and forms a big, spreading, informal mass of dense foliage. In the fall and winter female plants bear a profusion of bright-blue berries. Grows in partial shade or sun.

LAUREL, MOUNTAIN. *Kalmia latifolia.* Zones 5–8. Broadleaf evergreen. 30 feet. I rank mountain laurel on a par with andromeda, and in one respect it is better: as long as it gets a little sun, it flowers as profusely in shade as in full sun. It even grows well in rather deep shade but doesn't bloom.

Mountain laurel forms a big, rounded mound of green that isn't fazed by winter cold. In spring it bears large clusters of exquisite Chinese-bowl-shaped flowers ranging from white to pink to a warm red in the very newest varieties. In a good year the flowers are so numerous that you can hardly see the leaves.

LEUCOTHOE, DROOPING. *Leucothoe fontanesiana.* Zones 5–9. Broadleaf evergreen. 6 feet. Leucothoe is a choice plant for a partially shaded area. The arching branches are clad with lance-shaped leaves that in late spring are weighted with drooping clusters of white, bell-shaped flowers.

MAHONIA, LEATHERLEAF. *Mahonia bealii.* Zones 7–10. Broadleaf evergreen. 10 feet. The leaves of this warm-climate shrub are leathery, gray-green and spiny-edged and project stiffly out from the vertical stems. The effect may not sound appealing but is actually striking. The shrub offers even more, however. It has clusters of sweet-smelling, lemon-yellow flowers in early spring and blue grapelike berries in summer. Partial or filtered shade is essential.

Mahonia lomariifolia. Zones 9b–10. Broadleaf evergreen. 12 feet. A truly dramatic shrub rated by many the best of the mahonias. It has innumerable upright stems that put out large compound leaves divided into glossy, spiny leaflets. In winter each branch is topped with big, upright spikes of yellow flowers, after which come powdery-blue berries. Needs partial to light shade.

MYRTLE, TRUE. *Myrtus communis.* Zones 8–10. Broadleaf evergreen. 15 feet. The true myrtle is a dense, rounded shrub with lustrous leaves that give off a fragrant aroma when crushed. Its white flowers and blue-black berries are unimportant. Partial shade or sun.

NATAL PLUM. *Carissa grandiflora.* Zones 9–10. Broadleaf evergreen. 15 feet. This large, attractive, thorny plant produces jasmine-scented white flowers more or less constantly and edible red fruits in the summer. Partial shade or sun.

OREGON GRAPE. *Mahonia aquifolium.* Zones 6–10. Broadleaf evergreen. 6 feet. If you want a colorful plant for a partially shaded location, try

Oregon grape. It has hollylike leaves that turn bronze or rich purple in fall and winter, yellow flower clusters in early spring, and in summer blue-black, grapelike fruits from which you can make jelly.

OSMANTHUS, HOLLY. *Osmanthus heterophyllus.* Zones 6b–10. Broadleaf evergreen. 18 feet. This is a dead ringer for the American or English holly except that it has blue-black berries in the fall. Rather insignificant yellowish flowers in summer have a nice fragrance. Grows in partial shade or sun.

PEONY, TREE. *Paeonia suffruticosa.* Zones 6–10. Deciduous. 5 feet. Despite its name, the tree peony is a shrub. Its white, pink, red, yellow or purple flowers resemble those of the common garden peony but are much bigger and more spectacular. They bloom in mid-spring. Use the plants as accents where they don't have to compete with other shrubs. They grow in partial shade or sun.

PITTOSPORUM, JAPANESE. *Pittosporum tobira.* Zones 8–10. Broadleaf evergreen. 15 feet. Used as a specimen plant or in with other shrubs, pittosporum always shows off to good advantage. The leathery leaves are arranged in rosettes. Creamy-white flower clusters in early spring have an orange-blossom fragrance. The greenish-brown autumn fruits split open to reveal orange seeds. Partial shade or sun.

PRIVET, JAPANESE. *Ligustrum japonicum.* Zones 7b–10. Broadleaf evergreen. 12 feet. This popular hedge plant can be used equally well as an upright shrub. Its leaves are dark green; white summer flowers are fragrant. Prefers sun but grows in partial shade.

RHODODENDRON, CAROLINA. *Rhododendron carolinianum.* Zones 6–8. Broadleaf evergreen. 6 feet. Rhododendrons have handsome foliage and beautiful flower clusters (in this case rosy-purple). They need shade for part of the day. For brief cultural directions, see under AZALEA.

RHODODENDRON, CATAWBA HYBRIDS. *Rhododendron catawbiense.* Zones 5–8. Broadleaf evergreen. 15 feet. Of all rhododendrons these are probably the most beautiful. The flowers are as large as 3 inches across and are borne in huge, rounded clusters. They come in many shades of white, pink, red, violet and purple.

RHODODENDRON, KOREAN. *Rhododendron mucronulatum.* Zones 5–10. Deciduous. 6 feet. The Korean rhododendron is one of the first plants to greet the spring, its rosy-purple flowers appearing at the same time as forsythia's gold.

SARCOCOCCA, DWARF. *Sarcococca hookeriana humilis.* Zones 7–10. Broad-leaf evergreen. 3 feet. Slow-growing, spreading plant often used as a ground cover but equally useful in the front of shrubbery plantings. Glossy foliage and inconspicuous white, fragrant flowers in early spring. The shrub needs partial shade and will thrive in full shade.

SKIMMIA, REEVES. *Skimmia reevesiana.* Zones 7b–10. Broadleaf evergreen. 2 feet. An excellent small shrub, skimmia has dark-green leaves that are aromatic when crushed, fragrant white flowers in mid-spring and red berries in the fall. Must have partial shade.

STEPHANANDRA, CUTLEAF. *Stephanandra incisa.* Zones 6–8. Deciduous. 7 feet. This is the large version of the ground cover listed earlier. It has graceful arching branches and triangular leaves chiseled to suggest tiny fern fronds. Partial shade or sun.

SUMMERSWEET. Also called Sweet Pepperbush. *Clethra alnifolia.* Zones 4–7. Deciduous. 8 feet. Tight little clusters of fragrant white flowers give summersweet its name. A spreading plant, it eventually forms a large clump if it gets sufficient moisture. Grows in partial shade or sun.

TAMARISK, KASHGAR. *Tamarix hispida.* Zones 6–9. Deciduous. 6 feet. Tamarisk is a slender, upright shrub with leaves so minute they are visible only when you examine the stems close up; from a distance they give the entire plant a delightful silvery sheen. The deep-pink flowers in summer form huge plumes that swathe the plant like cotton. Partial shade or sun.

VIBURNUM. The large viburnum family includes a number of shrubs

The branches of the doublefile viburnum are clad from tip almost to base with white flowers.

that experienced gardeners call superlative because of their big clusters of white or faintly pink spring flowers, equally large clusters of fall berries and over-all shapeliness and good foliage. The best are listed below.

While all viburnums do best in full sunlight, they also show off to advantage in partial shade. Once established, they require little attention.

Burkwood viburnum. *Viburnum burkwoodii.* Zones 6–10. Deciduous. 6 feet. Very fragrant flowers. Black berries. Leaves turn wine-red in autumn.

Doublefile viburnum. V. *plicatum tomentosum.* Zones 5–10. Deciduous. 9 feet. Flat clusters of unusual white flowers cover the horizontal branches from the tip almost to the base. Berries turn from red to black. Purple-red fall foliage.

Fragrant Snowball viburnum. V. *carlcephalum.* Zones 6–10. Deciduous. 9 feet. Very fragrant flowers. Red berries turn black. Glossy foliage. Many people rate it higher than the following, which is one of its parents.

Korean Spice viburnum. V. *carlesii*. Zones 5–10. Deciduous. 5 feet. Extremely fragrant flowers. Blue-black berries.

Leatherleaf viburnum. V. *rhytidophyllum*. Zones 7–10. Broadleaf evergreen. 9 feet. Big leathery leaves. Yellowish-white flowers. Berries turning from red to black.

Siebold viburnum. V. *sieboldii*. Zones 6–9. Deciduous. 10 feet. Creamy-white flowers. Berries start out light red and gradually turn dark red and then black.

Tea viburnum. V. *setigerum*. Zones 6–10. Deciduous. 12 feet. Few plants have such spectacular fruit. The berries are big, glossy, bright red and hang in large clusters. Variety *aurantiacum* has equally brilliant orange berries.

Wright viburnum. V. *wrightii*. Zones 6–9. Deciduous. 9 feet. Of special value for its big clusters of very shiny red fruits.

YEW, JAPANESE. *Taxus cuspidata*. Zones 5–10. Needled evergreen. 25 feet. The dense dark-green Japanese yews are almost indispensable in the garden, and they come in enough shapes and sizes so it's easy to find just the right variety for any situation. The female plants have bright-red berries. Grows in sunlight or filtered, dappled or partial shade. Also takes complete shade if not too heavy, but the foliage loses some of its density.

YEW, SPREADING ENGLISH. *Taxus baccata repandens*. Zones 6b–10. Needled evergreen. 3 feet. The English yew bears a close resemblance to the Japanese yews except that it's smaller and has spreading, somewhat pendulous branches.

YEW PINE, SHRUBBY. *Podocarpus macrophyllus maki*. Zones 8–10. Broadleaf evergreen. 10 feet. The shrubby yew pine is a beautiful, useful, upright shrub with 4-inch-long, needlelike leaves. Partial shade or sun.

Planting trees. There are only a few trees that grow in shade, and there are only a few shady situations that call for trees. So you may not have any use for shade-tolerant trees. But if you do, rest assured that you won't be disappointed with the following. Every one of them is a prize.

Selected Trees for Shady Areas

ARBORVITAE, AMERICAN. *Thuja occidentalis.* Zones 6–10, but will grow as far north as Zone 2 if you don't mind its brown winter coloration. Evergreen. 60 feet. The tiny leaves are arranged in graceful fanlike sprays. The tree grows into a slender column that takes little space and stands out against the sky. Prefers sun but tolerates partial shade.

DOGWOOD, FLOWERING. *Cornus florida.* This is such a borderline case that you'll find it listed for sunny areas in Chapter 10. It grows in dappled or filtered shade but is very reluctant to bloom.

DOGWOOD, JAPANESE. *Cornus kousa.* Also described in Chapter 10.

FALSE CYPRESS, SAWARA. *Chamaecyparis pisifera.* Zones 3b–7. Needled evergreen. 120 feet. A gorgeous pyramidal tree with tiny needles arranged in dainty fernlike sprays. Use the tree as a specimen or in a tall hedge. Partial or filtered shade or sun.
   Variety *squarrosa,* known as the Moss False Cypress, is an excellent variation with feathery foliage of a definite bluish tinge.

FIG, WEEPING. *Ficus benjamina.* Zone 10. Broadleaf evergreen. 30 feet. A very ornamental small tree with pendulous branches clothed with glossy, leathery leaves. Sun or shade. Can be espaliered.

FRANKLINIA. *Franklinia alatamaha.* Sometimes identified as *Gordonia alatamaha.* Zones 6–10. Deciduous. 30 feet. This little-known tree has brilliant white flowers with yellow centers in late summer and fall. The large oblong leaves turn bright red in the fall. Sometimes the tree has flowers after the leaves have gotten their autumn color. Needs partial shade in warmest climates, tolerates it elsewhere.

HEMLOCK, CANADA. *Tsuga canadensis.* Zones 3–7. Needled evergreen. 90 feet. The Canada hemlock is one of our loveliest conifers, with short needles and slightly pendulous limbs that give it a feathery effect whether seen close up or from a distance. A fast grower, the tree will in time attain great size, but it can be held to compact dimensions by pruning. Prefers sun but does well in partial shade.

HEMLOCK, CAROLINA. *Tsuga caroliniana.* Zones 5–8. Needled evergreen. 90 feet. Under close examination there are distinct differences between the Carolina and Canada hemlocks, but from afar they look almost like twins.

HOLLY, LUSTERLEAF. *Ilex latifolia.* Zones 7b–10. Broadleaf evergreen. 60 feet. The lusterleaf holly is noted for its long, dark-green, lustrous leaves. In the fall, female plants bear large red berries in unusual tight clusters. The tree is more rounded than the American or English hollies. It prefers sun but grows well in filtered or partial shade. You must plant male and female specimens to have fruit.

IRONWOOD. Also called American Hornbeam and Blue Beech. *Carpinus caroliniana.* Zones 2–9. Deciduous. 35 feet. This is one of the few trees that actually prefer shade to sun. Its beechlike leaves turn orange or red in the autumn. The bark is smooth and blue-gray. But the prize feature of the tree is its twisted trunk and branches, which resemble heavily muscled forearms.

MAPLE, JAPANESE. *Acer palmatum.* Zones 6–10. Deciduous. 20 feet. The Japanese maple is our most highly prized small foliage tree. It has a delightfully irregular, Oriental-looking shape, with branches that sometimes weep. The leaves are finely chiseled and in some varieties resemble fern fronds. Depending on the variety, a tree may be a warm red throughout the growing season or it may start out red, turn green in summer and revert to red in the fall. For the best coloring, plant the tree in full sun. However, it will do and look very well in partial or filtered shade.

PITTOSPORUM, QUEENSLAND. *Pittosporum rhombifolium.* Zone 10. Broadleaf evergreen. 30 feet. This is a round, well-shaped tree with glossy leaves, little white flower clusters and very showy orange-to-yellow fruit clusters in fall and winter. Sun or partial shade.

Planting vines. As in the case of shrubs, there are few vines that require shade. But an overflowing handful do well in it.

Selected Vines for Shady Areas

	Deciduous or evergreen	Height (feet)	Climate zones	Comments
Actinidia, Chinese *Actinidia chinensis*	D	25	8–10	Vigorous, twining vine. Pretty white flowers turning yellow. Delicious brown fruits. Partial shade or sun.
Ampelopsis, porcelain *Ampelopsis brevi- pedunculata*	D	20	5–10	Climbs by tendrils. Fall berries change from lilac to yellow to bright blue. Partial shade or sun.
Creeper, Virginia *Parthenocissus quinquefolia*	D	60	4–10	Heavy, handsome clinging vine with big white flower clusters in spring. Shade or sun.
Creeping fig *Ficus pumila*	E	35	9b–10	Clinging vine. Young attractive little leaves become coarse, but pruning restores matters. All except very heavy shade.
Hydrangea, climbing *Hydrangea anomala petiolaris*	D	60	5–10	Climbs by tendrils. Nice on walls. Bright-red leaves in fall. Partial shade or sun.
Ivy, Boston *Parthenocissus tricuspidata*	D	60	3–10	Clinging vine, beautiful on walls. Very tough. Scarlet fall color. Partial shade or sun.

	Deciduous or evergreen	Height (feet)	Climate zones	Comments
Ivy, English *Hedera helix*	E	90	6–10	Clinging vine. Outstanding. Thick, dark-green foliage. Many good varieties. Does well even in deep shade. Also likes sun.
Jasmine, Confederate *Trachelospermum jasminoides*	E	20	10	Twining vine. Fragrant white spring flowers. Filtered to full shade.
Jasmine, Madagascar *Stephanotis floribunda*	E	20	10	Neat, elegant twining vine. Small waxy-white, very fragrant flowers. Partial or filtered shade.
Orchid trumpet vine *Clytostoma callistegioides*	E	20	9–10	Climbs by tendrils. Masses of orchid-colored trumpet flowers. Very adaptable. Shade or sun.
Wintercreeper *Euonymus fortunei*	E	25	4–9	Clinging vine. Fine leathery foliage, in some varieties variegated. Orange berries in fall. Filtered to light shade or sun.

Woodland gardens. A woodland garden sounds so easy to create that it's easy to understand why it should appeal—at least in theory—to many gardeners. After all, what is lovelier to walk through than open —emphasis on "open"—woods? But, unfortunately, to have a woodland garden you really need enough space so that when you are in the woodland you do not feel civilization pressing upon you. And to develop a woodland garden you need to be a better student of nature than most of us are.

By far the best woodland garden—and the easiest to make—is one that nature fashions for you without any assistance. You must cut paths through it so you can enjoy it, of course. You should remove plants, such as grapevines and bittersweet, that can turn the whole area into a shambles. And it's advisable to thin out the area just a little so you have better vistas through the trees. But let nature take its course otherwise.

Man-made woodland gardens are usually much less successful than

Two of the many forms of English ivy. The large-leaved upper plant is a glossy, bright green the year round. The smaller-leaved form is darker and has purplish tinges in the winter.

the natural kind, because even though the gardener puts in a wide variety of interesting plants, an artificial feeling pervades. The only way to avoid this is to spend a week or so studying the natural woodlands in your area and then try to emulate their best features with similar plants.

The alternative is to make the woodland garden a display area for rhododendrons and azaleas, or camellias, or a carefully worked-out mixture of the three plants. Such a garden bears little resemblance to reality.

But I have never seen anyone who didn't take delight in walking through an area crammed at ground level with these beautiful shrubs and shaded by tall trees spaced just far enough apart to let in ample sunlight.

Paving shady areas. Because ground covers, ferns and shrubs lend themselves so readily to filling in shady areas and require so little maintenance once established, there really isn't much excuse for covering the ground in such areas with crushed stone, gravel or chopped bark. It doesn't save much money or work, because the area needs to be raked regularly to keep it looking neat. It is not a surefire way to keep down weeds, although it helps a great deal. And it is not very attractive.

Yet I keep running across people who persist in the practice. If you must follow suit, please observe the following precautions:

Don't use white or very light-colored stones unless the area is frankly laid out and clearly identifiable as an informal terrace.

If the area to be paved more or less conforms with the shade pattern cast by trees, hills, buildings and other neighboring tall forms, use brown or dark-gray crushed stone or gravel that looks natural and blends into the landscape. Chopped tree bark and coarse peat moss are even better.

If the area is shaded by trees, do not under any circumstances place a layer of polyethylene film under the paving to prevent weed growth. This is often recommended as a good way to reduce garden upkeep, but it should be avoided around trees, because it deprives the roots of moisture and oxygen.

13 Improving Privacy with Fences and Hedges

Three questions must be answered before you undertake to improve the privacy of your house and lot.

1. What are you allowed to put up in the way of a fence, wall, hedge or informal planting to secure privacy? Time was when no one had to worry about this, but the situation is different today. For one thing, many communities have clauses in their building and zoning codes that limit the use of barriers around lots. As a rule, these do not restrict any sort of barrier less than about 4 feet high, but they frequently ban fences and walls that are taller than this in front of the house and perhaps also in back. Only tall hedges and shrubbery plantings are allowed. On the other hand, some communities allow fences and walls up to 6 feet high and even higher.

Other restrictions on what you erect may be contained in your deed. Again, these usually apply to very high barriers only, but in a few developments they may also apply to low ones.

2. Why do you want a barrier? Is it to give privacy from people wandering into your yard or to keep people from seeing in? The latter situation, of course, calls for a barrier at least 6 feet high—perhaps much higher if you don't want people to look down on you from a hillside or the second stories of their homes. But a low barrier—even one only 2 feet high—is adequate to keep people out, because even though they can climb over it, it says quite clearly "Keep out."

3. How will your next-door neighbors react? Many people don't care or would be in hearty agreement with your plan. But there are always some who take offense. This doesn't mean that they have a right to prevent you from doing as you wish. But they may turn cranky and disagreeable and make your life unpleasant in the future. This happens most often when a high fence or wall is built.

Obviously the only way to answer the question is to explain to your neighbor what you want to do and why, and ask for his reaction. If he gives you a go-ahead, you should then bring up the question of where the barrier is to be placed.

If you want to place it smack on a boundary line, it then becomes the neighbor's property as much as yours. Will he share in the cost of building it? Perhaps; perhaps not. Regardless of the answer, will he do his part in maintaining it? His immediate answer will probably be yes, but you can't be sure what will happen in the future. Maybe he'll get sick or lose interest, or maybe he'll sell his house to somebody else. In that case he may allow your fence to rot out from his side, or he may not trim a hedge, with the result that while your side is neat, his is tall and unkempt—and you don't have any right to cut his half.

Because a jointly owned fence, wall or hedge poses such problems, it is usually advisable to erect any barrier far enough in from a lot line so that you can get behind it to take care of it without trespassing on your neighbor's land. This, of course, reduces the usable area of your yard, and it may also mean that if you tire of caring for the barrier and let it run down, your neighbor will scream bloody murder. But this is preferable to the problems arising from joint ownership.

Which kind of barrier do you want? Hedges have natural beauty and can be as informal or formal as you like. It's even possible to change their appearance at almost any time. They stop wind more effectively than fences or walls. The least expensive type of hedge costs considerably less to put in than the least expensive fence, and in the long run it will cost even less. But maintenance is more demanding.

Informal shrubbery borders are more beautiful than most hedges or any artificial barriers, and they require considerably less upkeep. But while they are just as effective as wind-screens, they tend to cost more than hedges, and they take up a great deal more space. Most properties, in fact, are not large enough to accommodate shrubbery borders on the sides.

Walls are the most durable and the most handsome barriers. But the cost of construction runs so high that they have been losing ground steadily in recent years.

Fences have three outstanding virtues. They take up almost no space, give you instantaneous privacy, and can be designed in countless ways. Along with walls, they can be built to give complete privacy against intruders. But they are moderately expensive, require a moderate amount of maintenance, and usually have to be replaced in time. And for various reasons they have a faculty for stirring up controversy between neighbors.

Planting hedges. Since you want a hedge to make rapid growth, good soil preparation is essential. Follow the directions in Chapter 3, and be sure to mix in plenty of humus. The plants can then be set into a trench or individual holes. Trench planting is usually done when plants are closely spaced. In any case, take pains to set each plant properly: spread out the roots, and make sure it is upright before filling in around it with soil and watering well.

While they are young, evergreens need only enough pruning to keep them neat. But deciduous plants must be trimmed back regularly at the top to encourage them to make bushy growth at the base. The usual way of handling privet is to cut the small plants back one-third at planting, and then to cut them back 6 inches when they grow upward 12 inches. Repeat this process twice.

As noted in Chapter 6, as soon as hedges are well established you should start training them toward their ultimate size and shape. Take care not to let them grow too wide. Shear them so the sides are straight up and down, or better, slanting outward slightly at the base.

A fairly common way of treating evergreen hedges is to plant solid or semisolid fences close to them on the front side. This produces a delightful effect and helps to conceal the fact that the plants may not be well filled out at the base. Remember, however, that the fence screens the plants from the sun and kills most of the green growth directly behind

A hedge of Canada hemlock serves as a background for a simple white painted fence. Note that the hedge is kept narrower at the top than at the base in order to assure that the lower branches will not be shaded out.

it. As a result, if you should ever want to remove the fence, you would also have to remove the hedge, because the lower part will be black and threadbare.

Tall Hedge Plants to Keep People from Looking into Your Lot

	Deciduous or evergreen	Climate zones	Sun or shade	Height range (feet)	Space between plants (feet)
Arborvitae, American *Thuja occidentalis*	E	6–10	Either	8–30	2
Box, common *Buxus sempervirens*	E	6b–10	Either	3–20	1½–3

	Deciduous or evergreen	Climate zones	Sun or shade	Height range (feet)	Space between plants (feet)
False cypress, Sawara *Chamaecyparis pisifera*	E	3b–7	Either	10–30	4
Hemlock, Canada *Tsuga canadensis*	E	3–7	Either	8–30	3
Hibiscus, Chinese *Hibiscus rosa-sinensis*	E	9–10	S	6–16	3
Holly, American *Ilex opaca*	E	6–9	S	4–30	4
Maple, hedge *Acer campestre*	D	5b–8	S	12–25	6
Myrtle, true *Myrtus communis*	E	8–10	Either	6–15	4
Osage orange *Maclura pomifera*	D	5–9	S	10–30	5
Osmanthus, holly *Osmanthus heterophyllus*	E	6b–10	Either	6–18	3
Pittosporum, Japanese *Pittosporum tobira*	E	8–10	Either	4–30	3
Privet, California *Ligustrum ovalifolium*	D	6–10	S	3–15	1
Privet, Japanese *Ligustrum japonicum*	E	7b–10	S	4–12	1½
Russian Olive *Elaeagnus angustifolia*	D	2–9	S	10–20	5
Tallhedge *Rhamnus frangula columnaris*	D	2–8	S	10–15	3
Tea tree, Australian *Leptospermum laevigatum*	E	9b–10	S	10–30	4
Yew, Hicks *Taxus media hicksii*	E	3–10	Either	6–30	2½
Yew pine, shrubby *Podocarpus macrophyllus maki*	E	8–10	Either	4–10	2½

Low Hedge Plants to Keep People Out

	Deciduous or evergreen	Climate zones	Sun or shade	Height range (feet)	Space between plants (feet)
Barberry, box *Berberis thunbergii minor*	D	5–9	Either	1½–3½	1
Barberry, Japanese *Berberis thunbergii*	D	5–9	Either	3–7	2
Barberry, wintergreen *Berberis julianae*	E	6–9	Either	3–6	1½
Box, edging *Buxus sempervirens suffruticosa*	E	6–8	Either	1½–4	1
Box, Korean *Buxus microphylla koreana*	E	5b–10	Either	1½–4	1
Cinquefoil, shrubby *Potentilla fruticosa*	D	3–10	S	1–4	1½
Cotoneaster, spreading *Cotoneaster divaricata*	D	6–10	S	3–6	2
Elaeagnus, thorny *Elaeagnus pungens*	E	7b–10	Either	4–12	3
Euonymus, compact winged *Euonymus alatus compactus*	D	3b–8	Either	4–6	2
Euonymus, evergreen *Euonymus japonicus*	E	8–9	Either	4–15	3
Firethorn, Laland's scarlet *Pyracantha coccinea lalandei*	E or D	6b–10	Either	4–10	3
Hawthorn, yeddo *Raphiolepis umbellata*	E	7b–10	Either	4–10	3
Holly, Burford *Ilex cornuta burfordii*	E	7b–10	S	5–8	2
Holly, convex Japanese *Ilex crenata convexa*	E	6–10	Either	2–20	2
Hypericum, Hidcote *Hypericum patulum Hidcote*	E	6b–10	S	1½–3	1½

The beginning of a semicircular oleander hedge designed to shield the large window from the nearby street. The plants bordering the window are yew pines.

	Deciduous or evergreen	Climate zones	Sun or shade	Height range (feet)	Space between plants (feet)
Natal plum *Carissa grandiflora*	E	9–10	Either	4–15	3
Ninebark, eastern *Physocarpus opulifolius nana*	D	2–8	S	1½–9	1
Pine, mugo *Pinus mugo mughus*	E	2–9	S	2–8	2
Quince, flowering *Chaenomeles speciosa*	D	5–10	S	4–8	2
Rose, shrub *Rosa species*	D	4–10	S	3–8	2
Sarcococca, dwarf *Sarcococca hookeriana humilis*	E	7–10	Sh	1½–3	1
Skimmia, Reeves *Skimmia reevesiana*	E	7b–10	Sh	1½–2	1
Stephanandra, cutleaf *Stephanandra incisa crispa*	D	6–8	Either	2–3	2
Yew, Japanese *Taxus cuspidata*	E	5–10	Either	3–25	2

Planting informal shrubbery borders for privacy. The procedure is the same as that followed in planting any other type of shrubbery border.

When selecting shrubs, remember that privacy is needed in the yard only during warm weather; therefore it is unnecessary to confine yourself to evergreens. Deciduous shrubs are just as effective, and they are often more desirable because they will not shade the yard and possibly the house in winter if allowed to grow naturally. By contrast, a planting of evergreens may require occasional hard pruning to let in the sun—and such pruning destroys the informal effect the border is supposed to give.

Building walls. Whether a wall is made of brick, stone or concrete blocks, construction is a time-consuming job, and I don't think

OPPOSITE

A high, white concrete wall screens this terraced and paved garden area from the neighbor's view and at the same time serves as a superb background for plants. The exotic, multitrunked, big-leaved tree is a seagrape.

A border thickly planted with a wide assortment of shrubs—many of them unusual—to give the owner pleasure and provide privacy from nearby neighbors.

this book is quite the right place to describe it in detail. But you should at least know what is involved.

Because of the difficulties of construction and dangers of blowdowns, I don't advise that you consider trying to build a wall more than 3 or, at very most, 4 feet high. Both brick and concrete-block walls must be at least 8 inches thick; stone walls held together with concrete should be 12–15 inches thick (not because they are weaker but because it is hard to get good building stones of smaller dimensions). Dry stone walls are much thicker. Eighteen inches is minimum if you're lucky enough to have very flat, rectangular stones. Two to 3 feet is better.

All masonry walls should be built up from a poured concrete footing laid at least 18 inches below ground—deeper in colder climates. The width of the footing should be twice the thickness of the wall, the depth no less than 8 inches. For a dry stone wall, simply dig a trench about 18 inches deep and a little wider than the wall, and fill it solidly with small and irregular stones and rubble that are not suitable for the wall itself.

To make sure the wall is straight, build it to a taut cord stretched between posts at the ends of the wall. As each new course is laid, check with a carpenter's level whether the wall is straight up and down.

In constructing a wall, build up the two ends first, then fill in between them. In this way the ends are always a course or two higher than the middle.

Building fences. Two points about fence design should be noted.

1. On lots with a pronounced slope, tall, more or less solid fences designed to keep people from looking in usually look best if they do not follow the contours of the land. Build them instead as a series of steps.

2. If a tall fence is required not only for privacy but also to give protection against winds, it should not be built of boards or panels laid edge to edge, because the wind vaults over the top like a high hurdler and comes down within a few feet of the back side. Much better protection is provided if ½-inch or wider openings are left between boards or if large panels are pierced with closely spaced holes. Then when the wind strikes the fence, it tries to go through the holes rather than over the top; and when it emerges on the back side, its force has been dissipated.

Basket-weave fences like this are available from lumberyards and mail-order houses. The garden is planted with rhododendrons, andromeda, iris, lilies and peonies.

For maximum life, wood fences must be built only of rot-resistant wood. Natural woods falling into this category are redwood, cypress, red cedar and black locust (the last is used only for fence posts). But any other wood may be used if it is saturated with wood preservative. In all cases use lumber cut from the heartwood of logs rather than from the sapwood. Heartwood is more decay-resistant.

Plywood is also treated with a preservative. But in addition, you must make certain to use exterior-grade plywood—never an interior grade, which will delaminate. Other materials that may be used in large panels in fences include asbestos-cement board, fiber-glass-reinforced polyester and plate glass (or better still, safety glass).

Steel fencing should be galvanized. Ornamental fences made of ordinary steel or wrought iron need to be well protected with paint; even so, they rust out.

Nails, screws, bolts, angle irons and other fastenings must also be made of galvanized steel or brass, bronze or aluminum, because no matter how well you countersink, putty over and paint bright steel nails and other hardware, they eventually rust, stain the surface of the fence and disintegrate.

Posts for a fence are usually made of 4-by-4-inch timbers or 4-inch-diameter rounds. Normal spacing between posts is 8 feet, although this can be increased to 10 feet if the fence is very open or is not exposed to heavy wind. On the other hand, 6-foot spacing is preferred if you build a solid fence in a very windy location.

The post holes should be 30 inches deep. A post-hole digger—either powered by hand or by motor—cuts excavation time. If the posts are to be set in concrete, use a spade to widen the upper 12 inches of each hole to 12–15 inches diameter.

Use a taut line to position the holes. First mark the location for one of the end holes with a stake. Then measure along the line to the next hole, next, and so on, to the other end of the fence.

Before setting the posts pour 3–6 inches of gravel or small stones into each hole and tamp it well. (The heavier the soil, the thicker the gravel layer should be.) Then cut the posts to the proper height. Set the two end posts first. Have a helper hold them upright and check them with a carpenter's level. Then fill in around each post gradually with gravel. Firm this repeatedly with a 2-by-4.

Concrete is needed around the posts only if the fence is exposed to wind or traffic (alongside a sidewalk, for example). Fill the holes to within a foot of the surface with well-tamped gravel, and pour the concrete on top. Make the concrete of 1 sack of Portland cement, 2¼ cubic feet of sand and 4 cubic feet of coarse aggregate (clean pebbles no more than 1½ inches in diameter). As you pour the concrete, work a spade up and down in it to eliminate air pockets.

When the end posts are in place, stretch a tight line from one to the other just below the top and stretch a second line about a foot above the ground. Nail the cords to the sides of the posts. Then set the inter-

A fence of rigid, translucent plastic panels bars the view but allows light to shine through. Plants and structures on both sides are seen in silhouette from the opposite sides.

mediate posts so that they just touch the lines at top and bottom. Check the posts with a carpenter's level several times as you fill in around the bases to make sure they don't slant toward the end posts. When you nail the rails to the posts and the pickets or the panels to the rails, have your helper brace the posts upright.

Fences are made in many designs. A few are illustrated. All horizontal surfaces that face upward should be beveled slightly so moisture cannot stand on them. For example, the upper surfaces of rails should be slanted away from the pickets or panels. Similarly, the tops of pickets and panels should be beveled or covered with a horizontal cap strip that is beveled.

Instead of paralleling the ground, this fence is stepped down the hill. It is the best way to handle very high fences and those on small properties near the house.

To avoid incurring your neighbors' wrath, try to make the back of the fence as attractive as the front. Use as few braces as possible, or better, design the fence so the back matches the front.

Finish the fence with two coats of a penetrating oil stain to minimize upkeep.

Training plants on walls and fences. Walls and fences that are well designed and built don't need any decoration, but if they are so large that they look monotonous, you might consider training plants on them. (You might also train plants on the walls of buildings.)

The easy way to do this is simply to cover the wall with vines. On fences use vines that grow by twining or by means of tendrils. These can be anchored to the fence with nails and strings or by stretching galvanized or aluminum wires across the fence and letting the vines make their own way along these. The same sort of vines should be used on masonry walls that are painted. But on unpainted walls you can also use vines that cling to vertical surfaces by means of tenacious little aerial rootlets called holdfasts.* The latter are allowed to grow wherever they like; trying to pin them down to a prescribed route is almost hopeless.

---

* The reason for using this type of vine only on unpainted walls is that they are hard to pull down from painted walls and fences when these need to be refinished.

A more difficult but in many ways more rewarding way to decorate walls and fences is to espalier plants against them. An espalier is an ordinary plant that is, in effect, flattened out against a vertical surface and trained in a decorative, two-dimensional pattern. You can use either shrubs or small trees that have fairly small, supple branches: for example, firethorns, yews, apples, pears, podocarpus, hollies and magnolias.

A few nurseries sell plants that they have developed as espaliers. But you can develop your own espaliers and have a good deal of fun in the

An espaliered fruit tree against the side of a house. The garden is protected from the road by a curving, fan-shaped brick wall (left) and from the driveway by a picket fence.

A brick wall surrounding a circular garden area is clothed with ivy trained in a diamond pattern on wires.

process. After planting the plant about 6–12 inches out from the wall, select the branches that are growing in the desired directions and fasten them to the wall at about 1-foot intervals with string or insulated wires. Remove all the remaining branches and nip out unwanted buds and twigs on the espaliered branches. Continue doing this until the espalier has grown to the shape and size you want. From then on, remove the tips of the branches to limit further development, and cut out the unnecessary growths below. Also to limit growth, give the plant very little fertilizer.

The major pruning and shaping of an espalier should be done in the early spring. Minor pruning is done whenever it is called for.

14 Building a Terrace

I'd never go so far as to say that remodeling the garden is a waste of time unless you have a comfortable place in the garden where you can sit and enjoy the beauty you've created. But it comes close.

There are few things so soul-satisfying as relaxing on a terrace or deck on a balmy day and soaking in the light and color and texture and fragrance and sounds with which an attractive garden abounds. That alone is sufficient reason for building an outdoor living area. But there are many others.

A terrace is almost essential to casual summer entertaining.

It's a delightful place to eat (and also serves as the background against which the man of the house can display his culinary prowess).

It provides a safe, easy-to-watch-over play area for children.

It's the ideal setting for sunbathing and stargazing.

And if well designed, a terrace becomes the extension of the room off which it opens and makes the outdoors visually part of the indoors.

I for one am crazy about terraces, and in the three homes my wife and I have owned we have been lucky enough to have seven—three at the first house, one at the second, and three again today. Admittedly, this wealth of riches stems from the fact that we have always lived out in the country, where there was enough space for special terraces for eating and sunbathing plus an all-purpose terrace for anything else we wanted to do. This is a superlative arrangement, because it permits the same sort

Although they were only a few years old, this house and garden were extensively remodeled when purchased recently. Among the new additions was a mammoth flagstone terrace overlooking a magnificent view. Note the huge "imported" boulder and Japanese pine that break the monotony of the solid wall area.

of specialization and privacy that are afforded by the different rooms in the house and it also allows you to change outlooks and backgrounds to suit your moods. But the number of terraces you own is not nearly so important as just having one.

Where to put it. Establishing the perfect location for a terrace for an existing house borders on the impossible unless it was planned (but not built) when the house was put up and the garden developed. Some compromise is inevitable. But to reach a good compromise requires study. A number of factors influencing location must be considered and weighed against one another.

Privacy. Years ago one of our favorite couples owned a house with a big, luxurious terrace within 5 feet of the side lot line; and just 5 or 6 feet beyond the line was the neighbor's terrace. There was a hedge between the two, but outside of serving as a visual screen, it was no more useful than a veil. When each family had guests, voices grew louder, conversations became confused (but very careful, as a rule), and frequently some guest on one terrace would recognize the voice of a guest on the other terrace, and then the talk flowed back and forth, and on one occasion, over the protests of our friends, the parties actually merged.

Privacy doesn't mean a thing to some people, but to most it is rather precious. That's why it's one of the first things to strive for when locating a terrace.

On most properties the backyard is the first choice because it is concealed and buffered from the street. If the terrace is placed against the back wall of the house and more or less equidistant from the side boundaries, it is as far from the neighbors as you can get it. Finally—although this has nothing to do with privacy—it is surrounded by the largest and presumably the prettiest part of the yard and garden.

A terrace on the side of the house or on the back close to the side is

Because the ground falls away rather sharply to a river beyond, this terrace was necessarily set several feet below the house. But the big window brings it, in effect, right into the living room.

desirable only if you own an unusually wide lot and if your house is off-centered in it. Even so, while you may have ample privacy from the house next door, you lose the protection of your own house from the street.

Although few families give any thought at all to a front-yard terrace, the location is not without merit. To be sure, you may feel as if you're living in the middle of the street even though you surround the terrace with a high fence. But you may well feel further removed from your neighbors than if you put the terrace in the backyard. (This is especially true if your neighbors have their terraces in their backyards.) And if your house is perched on a steep hillside looking down at the street, a front-yard location may be ideal, because you're out of sight of the property bordering your rear boundary and you are almost out of sight of the street and the property on the other side. The only people you have to worry about are those on either side—and they are usually a problem only if their terraces are in the front yard too.

Accessibility. If you build just one terrace, you don't want it to be accessible only through a bedroom or bathroom. I doubt that anyone will argue that point. That means that it has to be accessible through the living room, family room, study, dining room, kitchen or—best of all— a central hall. Which will it be? With one exception, it doesn't really matter.

The exception is the kitchen. Despite the emphasis so many people put on eating and cooking on the terrace, that is not the real reason that it's often mated with the kitchen. The truth is that the two are linked because most houses have only one door to the backyard and it opens from the kitchen. But when you force people to enter or leave the terrace only through the kitchen, you do the housewife a grave disservice. For one thing, if she's a fussy housekeeper, she hates to have outsiders see what a mess her kitchen is in now and then. More important, the stream of traffic disrupts all culinary operations.

Making the entrance to the terrace through the living room, family room, study or dining room causes heavy wear in those rooms and can upset activities, but these are minor problems in comparison with disruption of kitchen operations. And on the plus side, a terrace off the

The owner at first felt this 18-by-38-foot terrace was too big but changed his mind after his first party. Now he says it is just right. The tiny building at one end is an old well house. To keep people from falling off the edge of the terrace a wide border of ivy is planted around the top.

living area is far better for entertaining and adds greatly to the charm and apparent size of the living space.

But, you say, there isn't an outside door in the living area. So how do I get out to the terrace except through the kitchen?

The obvious answer is to install a new door. That's no trick at all. Since windows in the living area are usually the same width as doors and are installed at the same height, the simplest solution is to remove a window, knock out the wall below it and set a door with glass insets (to admit light) in its place. Lacking a well-placed window, you can still put in a door by cutting an opening anywhere in a wall and installing a hinged door. It's even easy for a carpenter to knock out an entire wall and replace it with sliding glass doors, which, in effect, bring the terrace right into the house.

The sun. Except in hot climates, a terrace on the south side of the house is best, because it's exposed to sunlight for the better part of the day on all days of the year. Thus you get maximum use out of the terrace. In midsummer, however, the heat and glare may make you long for a roof.

For hot climates a north terrace is best, because it gets less sun each day and is therefore relatively cool. But it is the last choice in other areas.

East and west terraces are about on a par and about midway between south and north terraces in desirability. The main drawback of a west terrace is that it becomes objectionably glary in the late afternoon and evening as the sun goes down. On the other hand, an east terrace is sunny and warm in the morning, when you have least use for it.

Wind. Even in the tropics, wind is no friend of terrace occupants; hence the importance of placing the terrace—if possible—in the lee of the house. Of course you can screen a terrace with a high wall, fence or hedge, but even when properly designed (see Chapter 13), these must be placed so close to the terrace that they reduce the view and may impart a feeling of claustrophobia.

View. One of the few houses I know that is not oriented to the view is my family's ancient house in Mississippi. Despite a vast view

Few decks overlook such a view; on the other hand, most homeowners would think twice before building a deck 30 feet above the hillside, as this is built. The trees spearing up through the deck are encircled by holes large enough not to interfere with their growth and to permit the trees to sway in the wind without damaging the deck.

over the Mississippi River Valley to the west, the porch (1840 houses generally didn't have terraces) faces east to give protection against the wicked sun at the end of the day.

Today, it seems to me, views are so precious that almost every lucky possessor of one builds his terrace to enjoy it even though the sun or wind or something else is a nuisance. I'd do the same thing.

Contours of the lot. If your house is surrounded by flat or nearly flat land, the terrace can be placed anywhere. But a slope presents problems.

Let's assume that the best place for your terrace is behind the house. If the land at that point slopes sharply up, you must either build a deck off the second floor or dig back the hill and construct a massive retaining wall at the base in order to locate the terrace at first-floor level.

If the land slopes down behind the house from the first-floor level, you have a choice of either building a deck—if the slope is very steep— or building a retaining wall and filling in behind it with rocks, gravel and soil to make a terrace.

If the land behind the house is well below the first floor and slopes away from that point, you must also build either a deck or a raised terrace. In this situation, however, you can either build the deck or terrace where the land touches the foundation walls and put in stairs from the first floor, or you can build a deck at the first-floor level. Theoretically, you can also build a terrace at the first-floor level, but this requires such a high retaining wall and so much fill that the cost would be exorbitant.

In all these cases a deck costs less to construct than a terrace, but I have yet to see any deck that is attractive from all aspects. Some are exciting and delightful when you're sitting on them. But viewed from below the hill, even the best has a stark, structural look that is unsuited to a built-up neighborhood. For this reason a terrace is preferable. Consequently you may want to locate it on the side or in front of the house, where the wall-building-and-filling problem may be less difficult.

Terrace size. Unless a terrace is to be used for a single specific purpose—for example, sunbathing or dining—it's generally a mistake to make any smaller than your living room. For one thing, since it is in the open, it looks smaller than it actually is. For another thing, terrace furniture and activities take up more space than indoor furniture and occupations.

To be sure, some terraces are too big. This not only adds to construction cost and maintenance but actually makes for a vague but nonetheless real sense of discomfort in the occupants. I like to be able to sit on a terrace (as well as in a living room) and talk across it without feeling compelled to draw the chairs up into a tight little circle—and you can't do this on a terrace the size of a parking lot. I am also told by those who own them that an oversized terrace forces you to give oversized parties, because people in a small gathering feel lost. But there is no point in dwelling on these problems, because big terraces are the exception, not the rule.

I don't know what the perfect size is for a terrace. My friend Jackson Hand, the author of many books and magazine articles on construction, puts it at no less than 15 by 25 feet. I lean to anything from 16 by 16, which is quite a bit smaller, to 20 by 20, which is a little larger. But these are subjective opinions.

I am positive about two things, and I'm certain Jack agrees.

1. Regardless of the square footage, a terrace should be wide enough for practical purposes—that is, more than 10 feet. One that is narrower either makes the people using it string out in a long row so they can't converse or splits them into two groups at opposite ends. It also impedes traffic from one end to the other if you line up furniture on opposite sides. A more nearly square terrace is much better.

2. While a terrace surrounded with low walls increases seating space without requiring an abundance of furniture—people love to sit on walls—a terrace that flows uninterrupted into the lawn allows people to move off the terrace when it is crowded and still feel a part of the crowd. Put another way, a terrace surrounded by lawn at the same level can be made small enough to accommodate a small group but instantly expands to accommodate a large group.

Shape of the terrace. I don't know how much the trend toward building free-form and other oddly shaped swimming pools has influenced terrace designers, but just in case it has, let me start with a strong positive. The only reason to have a free-form terrace is that the contours or special features of a lot clearly call for it or that the designer is a good landscape architect. Otherwise use a geometric shape—a square, rectangle, circle, half circle or rectangle with bowed front. It's much easier to design: the do-it-yourself terrace builder is not likely to make any design errors. It's easier to construct. It blends better with the lines of the house and lot, which are almost always geometrical. It's simple—and in simplicity lies true beauty.

Paving. A number of questions enter into the selection of paving material for the terrace. What does it cost? Is the appearance suitable to the house and garden? Is it durable in your climate? Is it reasonably easy to maintain? The answer depends not only on the qualities of the material but also on the surroundings. For example, if you live at the seashore, you should use a very smooth-surfaced material to simplify removal of sand.

Will the terrace be exposed to a great deal of sunlight? If so, you should avoid a very light-colored material, which will be glary, and a very dark-colored material, which will soak up and hold heat. On the other hand, if you want to use a terrace in winter, dark paving is good, because it helps to warm you.

Will the terrace be in heavy shade? In a damp climate, shade encourages the growth of moss on the paving. And some materials, such as brick and wood, rapidly acquire a coating that makes them very slippery when wet—and very treacherous.

If the terrace is to be used for children's play, is the paving smooth enough not to skin their knees and allow them to roll their toys?

If the terrace is closely surrounded by trees and large shrubs, can water and oxygen seep through the paving to the roots? In other words, does the paving form a solid, tight sheet? If it does, the trees and shrubs may die.

Paving materials suitable for a terrace are described in the next chapter. They are brick, conventional concrete, exposed aggregate concrete, concrete patio tiles, ceramic tiles, flagstones, slate, cut stone blocks and wood blocks. Two other possibilities are artificial turf and indoor-outdoor carpet.

There are several types of artificial turf, but the best for terraces is

Potted plants are made to order for decorating terraces, whether these are paved solidly or in irregular flagstones separated by grass.

AstroTurf's Action Surface. This is the same material used in football stadiums and closely resembles bent grass. The blades are very green, soft, slender, short and dense. Installation is made over a base of concrete or blacktop. The resulting surface is comfortable underfoot, surprisingly durable and rather easily cleaned with a vacuum cleaner or hose. But it's costly and readily damaged by snow-shoveling and other hard usage.

Acrylic is the only type of indoor-outdoor carpet that should be used —and even it isn't very good, because it shows dirt and stains and is hard to clean. Easily damaged and worn, it generally needs to be replaced every ten years. And it soaks up rains and dries out slowly.

Building a deck. The main purpose of a deck—the modern version of a wooden porch—is to permit construction of a level outdoor living area on a slope that is too steep to be filled in for a terrace. Decks are also recommended for very irregular ground, ground projecting over a stream or pond, a sandy beach where a terrace is difficult to keep free of blowing sand, or at the second-floor level of a house. For how to build a deck, see Chapter 8.

Making a deck or terrace safe. Railings for decks are commonly made of 2-by-3-inch timbers. The posts are bolted to the sides of the beams or joists below the deck floor and are spaced 4–6 feet apart. The top rail should be 30 inches above the floor, and one other rail should be installed 15 inches below the top rail. If you have small children, however, installation of a third rail is advisable. The alternative is to tack fine-meshed chicken wire to the railing.

In the past, formal terraces raised above the ground sometimes had iron or decorative wood railings, but today the usual practice is to extend the retaining wall supporting the terrace up above the terrace floor to a height of 18–24 inches. The wall thus serves as a seat as well as a railing.

Walls are often omitted around terraces that are raised less than 18 inches above ground, on the theory that a fall from this height is rarely fatal. Nevertheless precautions must be taken to warn terrace occupants when they get too close to the edge. One way to do this is to set large planters of the window-box type around the edges of the terrace. Another solution is to build 12–24-inch-wide planting beds in the terrace floor about a foot from the high edges and plant them with low-growing evergreens such as English ivy, pachysandra, dwarf boxwood or Heller's holly.

Planting on and around the terrace. Except for the kind of planting just described, planting on the terrace proper is usually limited to a small bed around a tree or boulder that projects up through the paving. In addition to being decorative, this serves the useful purpose of keeping people stumbling around in the dark from smashing into the obstacle. A narrow bed between the terrace and the house may also be advisable to conceal the foundations and the otherwise sharp corner line and to soak up water dripping from the roof. On the other hand, this can be a nuisance, because it may be damaged by children playing and because it traps debris or scatters it on the terrace floor.

Generally the best way to plant the terrace proper is with potted flowers and shrubs in large containers that are not easily knocked over by people, dogs and wind. This, in effect, brings the garden right onto the terrace, where you can enjoy its color and fragrance close up. Another advantage of pot plants is that they can be moved around whenever you wish to change the terrace decor. Furthermore, if the terrace is partially shaded, you can grow sun-loving flowers in the shady area simply by moving them out into the sun for several days to encourage bloom and then bringing them back into the shade. (Conversely, you can grow shade-loving plants on the sunny part of the terrace by moving them back into the shade for a few days.)

The best place for permanent planting is around the outer margins of the terrace, but unless it is meant for screening or to emphasize the lines of the terrace, don't overdo it if the terrace is level with the garden. Too many plants will interfere with the view in and out, prevent overflow crowds from moving onto the lawn, and clutter the terrace with leaves, twigs and wilted flower petals.

If the terrace is surrounded by a wall or raised above the garden, however, low planting outside the walls helps to minimize their height and soften their lines when viewed from the garden. Of equal importance, the wall serves as a backdrop for the plants, accenting their structure and texture.

In the case of a deck, planting under the raised edges is essential to

Ferns are tucked in under a high deck to fill the otherwise dark, ugly space.

conceal the black cavern, supporting posts and bare ground beneath the floor. But here again you should avoid overdoing, because if you completely hide the understructure, the deck will appear to be floating on top of the plants. This looks peculiar, to say the least. Use just enough shrubs, very small trees and tall ferns to obstruct but not obliterate. If the outer edge of the deck faces south, east or west, plants that thrive in partial shade can actually be planted several feet back under the floor.

15 Paving in the Garden

Since statistically-minded ecologists came up with the "fact" that 10 percent of Los Angeles County is now paved, I have often wondered what the comparable figure is for gardens throughout the country. Somehow I doubt that it is as high as 10 percent, yet there is no gainsaying the fact that when you add up the square footage of driveways,

This California garden was extensively remodeled to provide a more attractive, private setting for the house, but the owner made the mistake of not straightening the walk, which still wanders in from the street corner like a snake.

An arrow-straight front walk paved in flagstones set tightly edge to edge.

parking areas, terraces, swimming-pool decks and walks, the figure is high. And that's an added reason—if one is needed—why we should all give more thought to the selection of paving and its installation in the garden. There simply is too much unattractive paving.

The front walk of the garden illustrated on page 229 is an example. In the first place, it is grayish-white concrete—about as cold and harsh and artificial-looking a material for use in a garden as I can think of. In the second place, it wanders like a snake, without any relation to its surroundings or to the way people walk. Finally, it reaches the street at a busy corner where no one can park even for an instant to get out of his car or let out passengers.

When the garden was remodeled under the guidance of a landscape architect the walk should have been torn out and redesigned. It wasn't; so it remains a flaw in the landscape.

Walks. While I'm on the subject let me say that since most walks on the average residential lot are utilitarian, they should be as straight as possible but with rounded (not sharp right-angled) corners. This is the way people walk—in straight lines and by cutting corners. Curving and sinuous walks should be used only when the contours or features of the land require them—and that isn't very often on small lots.

All walks must provide safe footing. They should be firm, level and smooth yet skidproof. In warm climates walks to the front and back doors should have an incline of no more than 1½ inches in 1 foot. In cold climates the grade should be no more than half an inch in 1 foot. Other walks on the property may be steeper—but just a little.

The minimum width for a front walk is 3 feet. But for two people to walk abreast, this must be increased to at least 4 feet, and preferably 5 feet. The need for a wide, two-abreast walk increases with the steepness of the walk and the age and/or health of the persons who use it.

Back walks should be 2 feet wide at least; and this same width should be maintained for other walks over which garden tools and children's wheeled vehicles move.

Steps should be the same width as the walks in which they are incorporated. (However, steps up to the front and back doors are often much wider than the walks.) Each flight should have at least two risers but should not rise more than a total of 5 feet. In flights rising less than

Old railroad ties are excellent for steps in the garden but do not provide quite enough tread area to be completely comfortable and safe. (Photo by Warwick Anderson)

An unusual but effective way to allow people to climb up through a garden with high retaining walls. (Photo by Warwick Anderson)

30 inches, the minimum width of treads is 11 inches, the minimum height of risers 7½ inches. In flights rising 30–60 inches change these dimensions to 12 and 6 respectively. Uniform dimensions must be maintained throughout each flight and, if possible, in all flights in the same walk. All treads should be pitched one-eighth inch forward to permit fast drainage.

On slopes that are not steep enough for steps but too steep for a sloping walk, build stepped ramps. No flight should have less than three single risers or three paired risers. In all cases the maximum height of the risers is 6 inches. In a ramp with single risers, each tread is long enough for a person to put his feet on it three times. In a paired-riser ramp, a short tread is combined with each long tread.

General rules for all paving. 1. To prevent settling, heaving and cracking, all paving must be laid over a solid base. This is usually provided by digging out the ground 4 inches deeper than the thickness of the paving material (for example, 8 inches if you are laying a 4-inch concrete slab, 6 inches if you are laying bricks), firming it well with a tamper, and then pouring in 3 inches of bank-run gravel or small crushed rock plus a 1-inch topping of sand. To simplify construction of the pavement, the excavation should be dug 4–6 inches beyond all sides of the pavement.

2. For drainage, slope the paving one-eighth inch in 1 foot to one or both sides.

3. To lay out a paved area with straight sides, stretch strong white cords between stakes driven well into the ground. The cords should be used to mark not only the outlines of the paving but also its elevation.

Construct a large wooden triangle to help you make 90-degree corners. The sides should measure exactly 3, 4 and 5 feet.

Irregular and curving lines are laid out with a flexible garden hose. To hold the hose in place during construction, staple it to the ground with heavy wires bent into U's.

4. All loose paving such as gravel should be laid an inch or two below the adjacent surface so the paving material will not scatter. A curbing of metal, boards, bricks, or concrete should surround the paving.

Solid paving, on the other hand, is laid flush with or no more than one-quarter inch above the soil line in an adjacent lawn; thus you can trim the edges of the lawn with your mower. Where the paving adjoins

Gravel walks should be set below adjacent lawn areas to keep the gravel from scattering. In addition to stopping the grass from spreading into the walk, the bricks form a mowing strip that makes it easy to trim the grass edges during normal mowing operations and thus eliminates the need for clipping.

a planting bed, however, it should be raised about an inch to keep soil from drifting onto it from the bed.

5. The majority of paving blocks can be laid either in concrete or on sand. The latter construction is generally preferable because it is much easier for do-it-yourselfers, less expensive and more readily repaired. In appearance it is more informal, less rigid. And water and air can work down through to nourish tree roots. The one disadvantage is that weeds and grass may sprout in the joints. However, this can be prevented if the pavement is not close to trees and shrubs by covering the sand base with heavy polyethylene film.

Asphalt. Asphalt is strictly a utilitarian paving material, used primarily for driveways, but it is also excellent for children's play areas because it has some cushioning effect when they fall on it, stores up heat and dries off quickly after snow or rain. Pavement is constructed either by applying about 2 inches of blacktop (a factory-made mixture of asphalt and crushed stone) on the prepared base or by treating the base with alternate applications of liquid asphalt and sand. The latter paving has a pleasant medium-to-dark-gray color, whereas blacktop is generally jet black and less attractive.

If you are not covering a lot of territory, you can put down packaged blacktop yourself. Just rake it out on a well-firmed gravel (not sand) base and roll it down. But for any sizable installation, call in a reputable paving contractor and insist that he follow your state highway department's specifications for asphalt paving (you may get an inferior job otherwise). A contractor is also required to put down liquid asphalt and sand.

Brick. Brick is a superb paving material used for all types of surface and is popular in all parts of the country because of its great beauty and durability. Although most paving is made of conventional red or pink rectangular bricks, there are numerous other sizes, shapes and colors to choose from. The textures are variable; use only those that are

Brick is an outstanding paving material in gardens. The border bricks here are laid in concrete so they will not twist under weight; the center bricks are laid dry on a sand base. Ordinarily the border bricks are set vertically, without mortar.

rough enough to be skidproof but not too rough to sweep. However, even the best bricks become very slippery if installed in a damp, shady area where moss grows. Staining by oils, acids and other substances can also be a problem but is largely preventable if a new pavement is given a couple of coats of penetrating masonry sealer.

Although bricks are often laid in concrete, you can create an equally durable, more attractive pavement by setting them in sand without mortar. The work takes time and care but is relatively easy.

Before ordering bricks you must decide which pattern you will lay them in. Bricks that have a face measurement of exactly 4 by 8 inches can be laid dry (without mortar) in any pattern; but unfortunately the bricks most commonly available measure slightly less than 4 by 8 inches, and you can put these down dry only in some patterns, not all.

The simplest pattern is known as the running, or common, bond and can be constructed with bricks of any dimensions (but of course all the bricks in a single paved area must be of the same dimensions). In this pattern all the bricks run in the same direction, but those in one row overlap those in the adjacent rows by half their length. Thus the short, vertical joints in adjacent rows are staggered.

After laying a sand-and-gravel base, the first step in laying a brick pavement is to establish the edges. These should be made of bricks standing on end so they will not tilt or twist outward. However, where an edge borders a wall, the bricks can be laid flat.

To build the edges, scoop out trenches, set in the bricks and pack fill firmly around them. The bricks can be laid with the 4-inch sides parallel to the terrace. This reduces the number needed. But the edgings will be stronger if the bricks are laid with the 2-inch sides parallel to the terrace.

Once the edging courses are completed, rake the sand base smooth and tamp it firm. Sprinkle with water, if necessary, to compact the sand. The top of the base should be slightly less than 2 inches below the tops of the edging bricks.

Cut a 2-by-4 to fit across the narrow dimension of the terrace and cut notches 2 inches deep in the ends to fit over the edge bricks. Then, starting at one end of the paved area, place the 2-by-4 over the bricks on opposite sides and pull it forward about 15 inches to level the sand. Smooth sand into low spots that are left behind, tamp it lightly and level the strip again.

Now set in the bricks one row at a time. To cut those at the ends of rows, score them on opposite sides with a cold chisel, then hold the chisel on one of the lines and rap it with a hammer. Square off the cut ends with the chisel and by rubbing them against another brick.

All bricks should be set tightly together, end to end and side to side, so that you can barely slip a knife blade between them. To make sure they're level, check each row with a board. Pound down bricks that are too high; lift and sprinkle sand under those that are too low.

Then level another 15-inch strip of sand with your notched 2-by-4 and lay three more rows of bricks. Continue in this way to the other end of the terrace. Check about every third row with a carpenter's square or large wooden triangle to make sure it is perpendicular to the edging bricks. If it isn't, take up as many rows as necessary and relay them.

When the pavement is completed, sweep dry sand back and forth over it to fill the joints. Then remove the excess and hose the terrace down to settle the sand. Add more sand, as necessary, to fill open joints.

If the paving is to be coated with a sealer, it should be applied before the joints are filled with sand.

Concrete. Concrete is by far the strongest and most durable paving material and is therefore especially suitable for driveways and much-used walks. But in its usual state it is the ugliest of all materials because it is almost white or pale gray and shows every stain. However, the appearance can be greatly improved if the paving is colored or given a special texture (like travertine rock, for example). When this is done well, concrete is acceptable in any location and for any purpose. But it still isn't pretty.

Because concrete paving is extremely difficult to finish, don't try to lay it yourself. Hire a mason.

Exposed-aggregate concrete. This is conventional concrete paving with small pebbles, marble chips, granite screenings, and the like embedded in the surface to form an informal mosaic with a pronounced texture. The resulting pavement is very handsome, durable, non-glary, and although not resistant to staining, it doesn't show stains. On the other hand, it's a little uncomfortable underfoot, drains fairly slowly, and like all poured concrete, keeps water and air from penetrating the ground below.

Construction should be handled by a professional, but since the aggregate conceals imperfections in the concrete, you can probably do the work yourself.

The concrete should be poured in a 3⅝-inch* layer over a 4-inch base of gravel. Divide the paved area into 4- or 5-foot squares with a grid of redwood or cypress 2-by-4s. (Use all-heartwood lumber.) The grid should be built with the 2-inch-wide edges of the timbers facing upward. Cover them with masking tape to keep them from being stained by the concrete.

Buy a ready-mixed concrete or make your own of one sack of Portland cement, 2¼ cubic feet of sand and 3 cubic feet of coarse aggregate. After sprinkling the excavation with water, pour the concrete into one square at a time and spade it thoroughly to eliminate air pockets. Then with a 2-by-4 strike it off flush with the top edges of the timbers.

The exposed aggregate can be a mixture of materials or all of one kind —a monochrome or a mixture of colors. In all cases the individual pebbles or chips should be ½–¾ inches in diameter to give a uniform effect.

Scatter the aggregate over the soft concrete until the surface is evenly covered and almost completely hidden. Embed the aggregate completely in the concrete by patting it with the flat side of a 2-by-4. Then as soon as the concrete begins to dry and harden, brush it away from around the upper half of the aggregate with a fairly stiff push broom. At the same time hose it lightly to remove the film of concrete on the aggregate.

Cure the pavement for a week under damp burlap. Then wash it with a solution of 1 part muriatic acid in 9 parts water to remove whatever concrete is stuck to the aggregate.

Concrete patio blocks. Concrete patio blocks are precast concrete slabs made in several shapes, sizes, colors and textures. They are less expensive and more variable in appearance than the flagstones and slates with which they compete, but they are also more breakable and more susceptible to staining.

Lay the blocks, which are 1½ inches thick, on a 4-inch sand-and-gravel base that has been tamped and carefully leveled with a 2-by-4.

---

* The actual width of a 2-by-4 is 3⅝ inches.

The base should extend several inches beyond the edges of the paved area to prevent tilting and twisting of the outer blocks.

If the blocks are all of the same size and shape, you can start laying them from any side of the paved area and work toward the opposite side. Line the blocks up in rows or let them overlap as in a brick common bond. However, if you are using squares and rectangles in various sizes, you should work out a paper plan for the paved area before starting actual construction.

There are two ways to make sure that all the blocks are level. One is to check each one as you put it down with a carpenter's level and also with a long 2-by-4 laid across the adjacent blocks. The other method is to lay the blocks as carefully as possible, cover the entire pavement with a thin layer of sand, and then scrape off the sand with a long 2-by-4. Finally, pick up the blocks that are still covered with sand, dump the sand underneath and spread it out, and then replace the blocks.

Provide one-eighth-inch space between blocks. When the terrace is completed, you can coat the blocks with a penetrating sealer to help prevent staining. The final step in the construction process (whether or not you use sealer) is to sweep sand into the joints and settle it with water.

If the paved area adjoins a planting bed, place a curb of wood or rigid metal against the paving blocks to keep them from sliding sideways into the bed. The curb should be about 4 inches deep.

Flagstones. Flagstones are large, flat sandstones in grays, blues or browns. They are a favorite paving material for terraces and walks because of their beauty, skidproof texture and moderate resistance to staining. They are also fairly durable (but not suitable for driveways).

Flagstones are sold in cut squares and rectangles of several sizes and also in irregular, uncut pieces that are fitted together like the pieces of a jigsaw puzzle. You can also have stones cut to any size and shape you require. If you are using squares and rectangles in assorted sizes, ask the masonry dealer to work out a numbered plan for laying them. This adds to the cost of the stones but saves you time and labor in developing your own layout.

If you lay flagstones on a sand-and-gravel base, use 1½-inch-thick stones and follow the directions for putting down concrete patio blocks.

A city terrace paved partly with brick and partly with small cut-stone blocks laid in an intricate pattern of interlocking fans.

If flagstones are used as stepping stones in a walk or path, you should also use 1½-inch stones. Simply scoop holes out of the soil, drop in the stones and level them by shoveling soil or sand underneath.

Flagstones are also frequently laid in concrete, but the work is best left to a professional because of the problems involved in building a perfectly level surface that water won't stand on. The stones used need be only an inch thick. The mortar joints between stones are one-half inch wide.

Gravel, crushed stone, pebbles and marble chips. Included here are all small stones or stone bits that have been washed free of dirt and sand. For simplicity I call them all gravel. No other paving material is available in greater variety.

If you use gravel, you can have paving with an attractive, natural look or a very unnatural, dramatic look at low cost. The material doesn't stain or reflect light; it retards runoff and it allows moisture and oxygen to soak into the ground. But it has serious drawbacks. It must be raked to look its best, and even so, it is likely to become fouled with twigs, leaves, cigarette butts, and what have you. Large gravel is miserable to walk on; small gravel gets into your shoes; and all gravel poses a threat to children who fall on it. Weeds are difficult to eliminate. And the gravel is easily scattered into adjacent borders and lawn areas, where it may damage the lawn mower. This is a particular problem in the North, because snowplows and snowblowers scatter gravel in large quantities every which way.

Gravel is a second-best material for paving driveways, terraces and walks, but it is often used because of its economy. It's also used by some people because they think that simply by spreading it on the ground, they can have a pavement. This isn't so. Unless the soil is full of rock or coarse gravel, new gravel spread on top quickly sinks in out of sight when people and cars move over it after a rain. For this reason, if your soil is of normal or very fine composition, you must dig out the area to be paved to a depth of 6–12 inches and pour in a thick base of bank-run gravel or, if the soil is clay, big rocks topped with bank-run gravel.

To prevent growth of weeds, spread polyethylene film on the ground before applying the gravel topping. The film must be slit at frequent intervals to let water pass through. The alternative is to treat the base with a soil fumigant. This can be used, however, only in areas that are far from trees and shrubs. And it's well to remember that it is effective only for several months; thereafter you should treat the driveway a couple of times a year with Ammate.

To keep gravel from scattering, the paved area should be sunk at least an inch below the surrounding ground and should be surrounded with metal, wood, brick or other curbs. One homeowner I know of in the Chicago area surrounded his gravel-surfaced parking area with a 3-foot-wide, slightly concave strip of cobblestones pressed into the soil.

Gravel teamed with solid paving blocks. Terraces are sometimes paved this way and so are walks, but the problems normally encountered with gravel and those normally encountered with the second paving material remain unchanged. In other words, the only advantage of this kind of paving is that the blocks serve as a design element that enhances the appearance of the graveled surface. The blocks also usually serve as stepping stones, which make it easier to walk across the graveled area and minimize the need for raking.

Slates. Slates are very similar to flagstones: another superlative material for terraces and walks. They are a little smoother and less durable than flagstones but somewhat more resistant to stains. The colors of some slates tend to fade after long exposure to the sun.

Precut slates that are large enough for paving are not carried in stock by most masonry supply houses but can be readily secured from these houses. You can buy squares, rectangles, and irregular pieces in a variety of sizes, and you can also order slates cut to your special measure.

Use 1- or 1½-inch-thick slates if they are to be laid dry. Three-quarter-inch thicknesses are suitable for laying in mortar.

Cut-stone blocks. If you want an unusual pavement that is also unusually beautiful and durable, try these small cubes of cut granite, sandstone, and other stone. Their only drawback is that they are a little rough and irregular in shape and size; consequently the pavement is hard to sweep and takes time to lay. On the other hand, they afford excellent traction on driveways and sloping walks.

The blocks are laid like bricks. If you want to put them down in straight rows, the joints between rows should equal the difference between the widest and narrowest blocks; and the joints between the ends of the blocks should be of equivalent width. If you don't want straight rows, on the other hand, fit the blocks together as tightly as possible. This results in a crazy-quilt pattern that is often very interesting.

Tile. Quarry tiles, patio tiles and pavers are heavy-duty ceramic tiles made in numerous shapes, sizes, textures and gorgeous colors. Some tiles have special designs. All make a beautiful terrace floor that is highly resistant to staining and very easy to clean. But the tiles are fairly fragile and slippery when wet.

The largest tiles—those at least 9 inches square by three-quarters of an inch thick—can be laid on a sand-and-gravel base like concrete patio blocks. But the smaller tiles are too breakable and lightweight for dry installation and should be set in concrete by a professional.

Wood blocks. You can make your own wood blocks by cutting debarked logs or 6-by-6-inch timbers into 6-inch lengths. Use redwood, cypress or cedar or any other species of wood that's been soaked (after cutting) for several hours in wood preservative.

Paving made of square wood blocks is a warm brown color that blends with the landscape. It is pleasantly resilient underfoot and very quiet. But it is dangerously slick when wet, soaks up stains and is hard to sweep clean because dirt particles become embedded in the surface.

Round wood blocks make a less attractive and generally less satisfac-

Square wood blocks make an attractive, resilient, quiet pavement but are slippery when wet.

tory surface, because the big, irregular spaces between them must be filled with sand, crushed rock or concrete.

Lay a square-block pavement like a brick pavement. The blocks should be placed with the end grain facing up. Set the blocks together as tightly as possible; sweeping sand into the joints is unnecessary since the wood will expand and lock the blocks into position.

Appendix

ALABAMA	Auburn University, Auburn 36830
ALASKA	University of Alaska, College 99701
ARIZONA	University of Arizona, Tucson 85721
ARKANSAS	Division of Agriculture, University of Arkansas, Fayetteville 72701
CALIFORNIA	College of Agriculture, University of California, Berkeley 94720
COLORADO	Colorado State University, Fort Collins 80521
CONNECTICUT	College of Agriculture, University of Connecticut, Storrs 06268
	Connecticut Agricultural Experiment Station, New Haven 06504
DELAWARE	School of Agriculture, University of Delaware, Newark 19711
FLORIDA	University of Florida, Gainesville 32601
GEORGIA	College of Agriculture, University of Georgia, Athens 30601
HAWAII	University of Hawaii, Honolulu 96822
IDAHO	College of Agriculture, University of Idaho, Moscow 83843
ILLINOIS	College of Agriculture, University of Illinois, Urbana 61801
INDIANA	Purdue University, Lafayette 47907
IOWA	Iowa State University of Science and Technology, Ames 50010
KANSAS	College of Agriculture, Kansas State University, Manhattan 66502
KENTUCKY	College of Agriculture, University of Kentucky, Lexington 40506
LOUISIANA	Agricultural College, Louisiana State University, Baton Rouge 70800
MAINE	College of Agriculture, University of Maine, Orono 04473
MARYLAND	University of Maryland, College Park 20740
MASSACHUSETTS	College of Agriculture, University of Massachusetts, Amherst 01002
MICHIGAN	College of Agriculture, Michigan State University, East Lansing 48823
MINNESOTA	College of Agriculture, University of Minnesota, St. Paul 55101
MISSISSIPPI	Mississippi State University, State College 39762

MISSOURI	College of Agriculture, University of Missouri, Columbia 65201
MONTANA	Montana State University, Bozeman 59715
NEBRASKA	College of Agriculture, University of Nebraska, Lincoln 68503
NEVADA	College of Agriculture, University of Nevada, Reno 89507
NEW HAMPSHIRE	University of New Hampshire, Durham 03824
NEW JERSEY	Rutgers—The State University, New Brunswick 08903
NEW MEXICO	College of Agriculture, New Mexico State University, University Park 88070
NEW YORK	College of Agriculture, Cornell University, Ithaca 14850
NORTH CAROLINA	College of Agriculture, North Carolina State University at Raleigh, Raleigh 27600
NORTH DAKOTA	North Dakota State University of Agriculture and Applied Science, Fargo 58102
OHIO	College of Agriculture, Ohio State University, Columbus 43210
OKLAHOMA	Oklahoma State University, Stillwater 74074
OREGON	Oregon State University, Corvallis 97331
PENNSYLVANIA	Pennsylvania State University, University Park 16802
PUERTO RICO	University of Puerto Rico, Box 607, Rio Piedras 00928
RHODE ISLAND	University of Rhode Island, Kingston 02881
SOUTH CAROLINA	Clemson University, Clemson 29631
SOUTH DAKOTA	South Dakota State University, Brookings 57006
TENNESSEE	College of Agriculture, University of Tennessee, Knoxville 37900
TEXAS	Texas A. & M. University, College Station 77843
UTAH	College of Agriculture, Utah State University, Logan 84321
VERMONT	State Agricultural College, University of Vermont, Burlington 05401
VIRGINIA	Virginia Polytechnic Institute, Blacksburg 24061
WASHINGTON	Washington State University, Pullman 99163
WEST VIRGINIA	West Virginia University, Morgantown 26506
WISCONSIN	College of Agriculture, University of Wisconsin, Madison 53706
WYOMING	College of Agriculture, University of Wyoming, Laramie 82070

Index

$4.95

$5.75
in Cana

HOW TO REDESIGN
YOUR YARD AND GARDEN

Stanley Schuler, America's great yard and garden expert, shows you how your yard and garden can look totally renewed through following easy relandscaping procedures.

Contents

Hawthorn Books, Inc.
Publishers
260 Madison Avenue
New York, New York 10016

0–8015–3746